MW01002975

MENDOCINO
& REDWOOD COUNTRY

STUART THORNTON

Contents

THE NORTH COAST

The rugged North Coast of California is spectacular, its wild beauty in many places unspoiled and almost desolate. The cliffs are forbidding, the beaches are rocky and windswept, and the surf thunders in with formidable authority. This is not the California coast of surfer movies, though hardy souls do ride the chilly Pacific waves as far north as Crescent City.

From Bodega Bay, Highway 1 twists and turns north along hairpin curves that will take your breath away. The Sonoma and Mendocino coasts offer lovely beaches and forests, top-notch cuisine, and a friendly, uncrowded wine region. Along the way, tiny coastal towns—Jenner, Gualala, Point Arena, Mendocino, Fort Bragg—dot the hills and valleys, beckoning travelers with bed-and-breakfasts, organic farms and relaxing respites from the road.

Between the towns are a wealth of coastal access areas to take in the striking meeting of land and sea. Inland, Mendocino's hidden wine region offers the rural and relaxed pace missing from that other famous wine district. Anderson Valley and Hopland can quench your thirst whether it's for beer at the local microbrewery or wine at one of many tasting rooms. Where Highway 1 merges with U.S. 101 is the famous Lost Coast, accessed only via steep narrow roads or by backpacking the famous Lost Coast Trail. This is California at its wildest.

For most travelers, the North Coast means redwood country, and U.S. 101 marks the gateway to those redwoods. The famous, immense coastal sequoias loom along the highway south of the old logging town of Eureka and the hip college outpost of Arcata. A plethora

HIGHLIGHTS

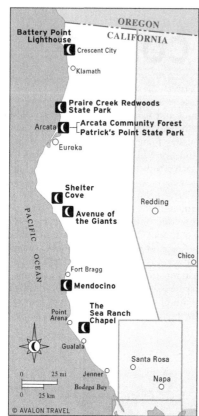

LOOK FOR ◖ TO FIND RECOMMENDED SIGHTS, ACTIVITIES, DINING, AND LODGING.

◖ **The Sea Ranch Chapel:** Embedded with seashells and sea urchins, this tiny place of worship and meditation is wholly unique (page 12).

◖ **Mendocino:** Spend an afternoon or a weekend wandering this arts-filled community and its headlands, which jut out into the Pacific (page 22).

◖ **Avenue of the Giants:** The towering coast redwoods in Humboldt Redwoods State Park are a true must-see. Simply gaze at the silent giants or head to the nearby Eel River for a quick dip (page 48).

◖ **Shelter Cove:** The Lost Coast is a section of the California shoreline like no other – wild and virtually untouched. This tiny town offers one of the best ways to see it with the lovely, relatively accessible **Black Sand Beach** (page 56).

◖ **Arcata Community Forest:** The first city-owned forest in California offers acres of trails winding through second-growth redwoods (page 69).

◖ **Patrick's Point State Park:** Replete with beaches, landmarks, trails, and campgrounds, this is one of the best of the many parks along the North Coast (page 74).

◖ **Prairie Creek Redwoods State Park:** With big trees, impressive wildlife, a long, lonely beach, and one-of-a-kind Fern Canyon, this park is worth a stop (page 79).

◖ **Battery Point Lighthouse:** This lighthouse on an island off Crescent City is only accessible at low tide. If you time it right, you can receive an insightful tour from the lighthouse keeper (page 85).

of state and national parks lure travelers with numerous hiking trails, forested campgrounds, kitschy tourist traps and some of the tallest and oldest trees on the continent. Pitch a tent in Humboldt Redwoods State Park, cruise the Avenue of the Giants, and gaze in wonder at the primordial Founders Grove. Crescent City marks the northern terminus of the California Coast, a seaside town known for fishing, seafood—and for surviving a tsunami.

PLANNING YOUR TIME

If you're planning a road trip to explore the North Coast in depth and want to make stops in more than one destination, plan to spend a full week. Driving is the way to get from place

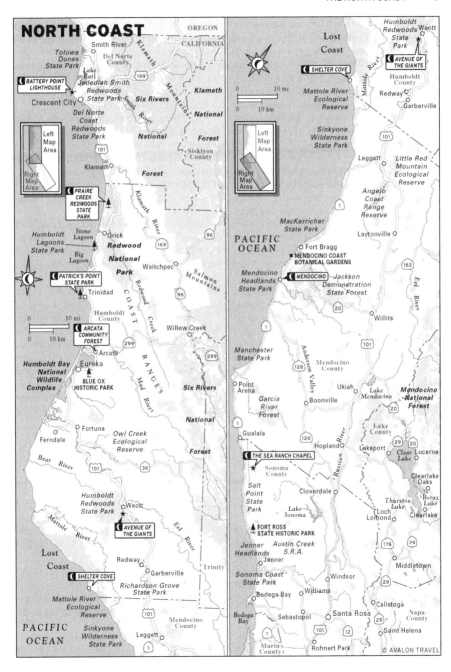

to place, unless you're a hard-core backpacker. Highway 1 winds along the North Coast from Bodega Bay to above Fort Bragg, where it heads east to connect with U.S. 101 at its northern terminus near Leggett. U.S. 101 then heads inland through southern Humboldt County before heading back to the coast at Eureka. North of Eureka, U.S. 101 continues through Arcata, Trinidad, and Crescent City, along with the Redwood National and State Parks.

If you are heading to Mendocino or a section of the coast north of there, take U.S. 101, which is a great deal faster than Highway 1, and then take one of the connector roads from U.S. 101 to Highway 1. One of the best and most scenic connector roads is Highway 128, which heads east off U.S. 101 at Cloverdale and passes through the scenic Anderson Valley, with its many wineries, before joining Highway 1 just south of the town of Mendocino.

Driving times on Highway 1 tends to be longer on the North Coast due to the roadway's twists, turns, and many spectacular ocean vistas. On U.S. 101 north of Leggett, expect to share the road with lumbering—pun intended—logging vehicles. A lot of the roads off U.S. 101 or Highway 1 are worthwhile excursions, but expect adventurous drives through mountainous terrain.

Many Bay Area residents consider Mendocino County ideal for a weekend getaway or romantic retreat. A weekend is about the perfect length of time to spend on the Mendocino coast or in the Anderson Valley wine country. (You might want to extend your trip for a day or two or three...) There are at least 3-4 days' worth of intriguing hikes to take in Redwood National and State Parks.

Along the Lost Coast, the most lodging and dining options can be found in Shelter Cove. If you want to explore the Lost Coast Trail, consider hiking it north to south, with the wind at your back. Spend the night in Ferndale or camp at the Mattole Recreation Site, where the trail begins, so that you can get an early start for the first day of backpacking.

Eureka is the biggest North Coast city, with the most amenities for travelers, so it makes a good base. If you're exploring the redwood parks, consider staying in the smaller towns of Arcata or Trinidad. The campgrounds at Patrick's Point State Park and Prairie Creek State Park are superb places to pitch a tent.

Summer on the North Coast has average daily temperatures in the mid 60s, which is comparable to the temps in southern California during the winter. Expect rain on the North Coast from November to May. The chances of fog or rain are significantly lower in the fall, making it one of the best times to visit. Frequent visitors to the area know this, so many popular hotels book up quickly for fall weekends.

Sonoma Coast

One good way to begin your meanders up the coast is to take U.S. 101 out of San Francisco as far as Petaluma, and then head west toward Highway 1. This stretch of Highway 1 is also called the Shoreline Highway. As you travel toward the coast, you'll leave urban areas behind for a while, passing through some of the most pleasant villages in California.

BODEGA BAY

Bodega Bay is popular for its coastal views, whale-watching, and seafood—but it's most famous as the filming locale of Alfred Hitchcock's *The Birds*. The town of Bodega Bay sits on the eastern side of the harbor, while Bodega Head is a peninsula that shields the bay from the ocean.

Whale-Watching

The best sight you could hope to see is a close-up view of Pacific gray whales migrating home to Alaska with their newborn calves. The whales pass this area January-May on their way from their summer home off Mexico. If

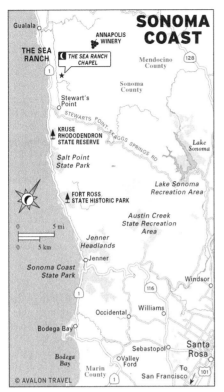

SONOMA COAST

sonoma-county.org, day use $7 per vehicle, camping $28-32). It is less than one mile down the road and worth the trip. You can even swim at Doran Beach; although it's cold, it's protected from the open ocean waves, so it's much safer than most of the beaches along the coast.

Sonoma Coast State Park

Seventeen miles of coast are within **Sonoma Coast State Park** (707/875-3483, www.parks. ca.gov, day use $8 per vehicle). The park's boundaries extend from Bodega Head at the south up to the Vista Trailhead, four miles north of Jenner. As you drive up Highway 1, you'll see signs for various beaches. Although there are lovely places to walk, fish, and maybe sunbathe on the odd hot day, it is not advisable to swim here. If you go down to the water, bring your binoculars and camera. The cliffs, crags, inlets, whitecaps, mini islands, and rock outcroppings are fascinating in any weather, and their looks change with the shifting tides and fog.

Events

The annual **Bodega Seafood, Art, and Wine Festival** (707/824-8717, www.winecountryfestivals.com, $12-15) combines all the best elements of the Bodega lifestyle. Taking place the last weekend in August, it includes live music in addition to tastings, special dinners, and much more. The proceeds help benefit two worthy organizations: the Bodega Volunteer Fire Department and Stewards of the Coast and Redwoods.

Accommodations

Bodega Bay Lodge (103 Hwy. 1, 707/875-3525 or 888/875-2250, www.bodegabaylodge.com, $300-610) is one of the more luxurious places to stay in the area. The rooms are located in seven separate buildings. If you really want to spoil yourself, secure an ocean club suite, which has a bedroom, private living room, and a private terrace with ocean views. The facility also has a spa, an ocean view pool, a fitness center, a fine restaurant, and a library on its grounds.

Sonoma Coast State Park (707/875-3483, www.parks.ca.gov, day use $8 per vehicle)

you're lucky, you can see them from the shore. **Bodega Head,** a promontory just north of the bay, is a place to get close to the migration route. To get to this prime spot, travel north on Highway 1 about one mile past the visitors center and turn left onto Eastshore Road; make a right at the stop sign, and then drive three more miles to the parking lot. On weekends, volunteers from **Stewards of the Coast and Redwoods** (707/869-9177, www.stewardsofthecoastandredwoods.org) are available to answer questions. Contact them for organized whale-watching tours or to learn more about their various educational programs.

Doran Regional Park

When you arrive in Bodega Bay, you'll see a sign pointing left for **Doran Regional Park** (201 Doran Beach Rd., 707/875-3540, www.

encompasses several campgrounds along its 17-mile expanse. Some of these have been casualties (let's hope temporarily) of the ongoing state budget crisis, but as of this writing, you can still get a lovely, sandy spot in the trees in **Bodega Dunes Campground** (2585 Hwy. 1, $35), complete with hot showers and flush toilets. To get up-to-date information on closings or re-openings related to Sonoma Coast State Park, call the **district office** (707/865-2391), or stop in at the **Salmon Creek Ranger Station** a little farther north.

Food

Go "wine surfing" at ◖**Gourmet au Bay** (913 Hwy. 1, 707/875-9875, www.gourmetaubay. com, Sun.-Thurs. 11am-7pm, Fri.-Sat. 11am-8pm, tasting $9), where they will pour three wines and lay them out on a miniature surfboard for you to carry out to the deck. Wines are available from a variety of different vintners, including major players in the Napa wine scene, small local wineries and the odd French or Australian vintage. Inside, you can sip as you peruse the gift shop, which includes local artisanal foods, handmade ceramics and pottery, and an array of toys for wine lovers.

Bodega Bay Lodge's **Duck Club Restaurant** (103 Hwy. 1, 707/875-3525, www.bodegabaylodge.com, daily 7:30am-11am and 6pm-9pm, $18-36) offers a warm and elegant dining experience featuring hearty American entrées like steak, chicken, and halibut with seasonal vegetables. There's a fireside lounge overlooking the bay, and even some outdoor seating for warmer days.

One of the best restaurants in the area is **Terrapin Creek** (1580 Eastshore Dr., 707/875-2700, www.terrapincreekcafe.com, Thurs.-Sun. 11am-2:30pm and 4:30pm-9pm, $22-29), where they make creative use of the abundance of fresh seafood available and cook up tasty pasta, duck, and beef entrées.

Information and Services

The **Sonoma Coast Visitors Center** (850 Hwy. 1, 707/875-3866, Mon.-Sat. 9am-5pm, Sun. 10am-5pm) in Bodega Bay may look small, but it's chock-full of exactly what you came for: maps, brochures, lists, suggestions, trail guides, events schedules, and even live advice from a local expert.

Getting There and Around

Bodega Bay is located on Highway 1 north of Point Reyes National Seashore and west of Petaluma. From the Bay Area, it's a beautiful drive north, hugging the coast, but the cliffs and the road's twists and turns mean taking it slow. A faster way to get here is to take U.S. 101 to Petaluma, take the exit for East Washington Street, and follow Bodega Avenue to Valley Ford Road, cutting across to the coast. You'll hit Bodega Bay just about two miles after you pass through Valley Ford. The latter route takes about 1.5 hours, with some of the route slow and winding.

JENNER

Jenner is on Highway 1 at the mouth of the Russian River. It's a beautiful spot for a quiet honeymoon or a paddle in a kayak. **Goat Rock State Beach** (Goat Rock Rd., 707/875-3483, www.parks.ca.gov, day use $8) is at the mouth of the Russian River inside Sonoma Coast State Park. A colony of Harbor Seals breed and frolic here, and you may also see gray whales, sea otters, elephant seals, and a variety of sea life. Pets are not allowed, and swimming is prohibited.

Accommodations and Food

Both the food and the views are memorable at ◖**River's End** (11048 Hwy. 1, 707/865-2484, www.ilovesunsets.com, summer daily noon-3:30pm and 5pm-8:30pm, winter Thurs.-Mon. noon-3:30pm and 5pm-8:30pm, $19-42). The restaurant is perched above the spot where the Russian River flows into the Pacific, and it's a beautiful sight to behold over, say, oysters or filet mignon. Prices are high, but if you get a window table at sunset, you may forget to think about them.

The **Jenner Inn and Cottages** (10400 Hwy. 1, 707/865-2377 or 800/732-2377, www.jennerinn.com, $118-358) has a variety of quiet, beautifully furnished guest rooms mere steps from the river. Some guest rooms have hot tubs and private decks, and breakfast is included.

Fourteen miles north of Jenner proper is the large and luxurious **Timber Cove Inn** (21780 N. Hwy. 1, 707/847-3231 or 800/987-8319, www.timbercoveinn.com, $182-300), with a spacious bar and lounge, an oceanfront patio, guest rooms with spa tubs and fireplaces, and hiking trails nearby.

Information and Services

The small but friendly **Jenner Visitors Center** (10439 Hwy. 1, 707/865-9757, www.steward-softhecoastandredwoods.org, summer Sun.-Thurs.) is located across the street from the Jenner Inn. The visitors center is staffed by volunteers, so hours can be unpredictable; call ahead to confirm.

Getting There and Around

Jenner is located on Highway 1, right along the ocean. There is no public transportation to get here, but it is a pretty drive from just about anywhere. The fastest route from San Francisco (about 1.75 hours) is to drive up U.S. 101, make a left onto Washington Street in Petaluma. Washington Street becomes Bodega Avenue and then Valley Ford Road before you make a slight left onto Highway 1 and head north toward Jenner. From Sacramento (2.5 hours) or points in the East Bay, take I-80 west and then navigate to Petaluma, where you continue west to Highway 1.

NORTH OF JENNER

As you hug the shore north of Jenner, you'll soon pass through Fort Ross State Historic Park, Salt Point State Park, and Kruse Rhododendron State Reserve.

Fort Ross State Historic Park

There is no historic early American figure named Ross who settled here; believe it or not, "Ross" is short for "Russian," and this park commemorates the history of Russian settlement on the North Coast. A quick rundown of the story: In the 19th century Russians

came to the wilds of Alaska and worked with native Alaskans to develop a robust fur trade, killing seals, otters, sea lions, and land mammals for their pelts. The enterprise required sea travel as the hunters chased the animals as far as California. Eventually, a group of fur hunters and traders came ashore on what is now the Sonoma Coast and developed a fortified outpost that became known as **Fort Ross** (19005 Hwy. 1, Jenner, 707/847-3286, www.parks.ca.gov, Sat.-Sun. and holidays sunrise-sunset, visitors center and fort compound Sat.-Sun. and holidays 10am-4:30pm, parking $8). The area gradually became not only a thriving Russian American settlement but also a center for agriculture and shipbuilding and the site of California's first windmills. Learn more at the park's large visitors center, which provides a continuous film and a roomful of exhibits.

You can also walk into the reconstructed fort buildings and see how the settlers lived. (U.S. 101 was originally built through the middle of the fort area, but it was moved to make way for the historic park.) The only original building still standing is the captain's quarters—a large, luxurious house for that time and place. The other buildings, including the large bunkhouse, the chapel, and the two cannon-filled blockhouses, were rebuilt using much of the original lumber used by the Russians. Be aware that a serious visit to the whole fort and the beach beyond entails a level but long walk; wear comfortable shoes and consider bringing a bottle of water.

Unfortunately, this park is one of the casualties of the state's ongoing budget crisis, so since 2011, Reef Campground is closed until further notice, and the park is open for day use only on Saturday-Sunday and holidays. It's still worth a visit, though—just call the **district office** (707/865-2391) before you go to make sure it's open.

Salt Point State Park

Stretching for miles along the Sonoma coastline, **Salt Point State Park** (25050 Hwy. 1, Jenner, 707/847-3221, www.parks.ca.gov, visitors center Apr.-Oct. Sat.-Sun. 10am-3pm, day use $8) provides easy access from U.S. 101 to more than a dozen sandy state beaches. You don't have to visit the visitors center to enjoy this park and its many beaches—just follow the signs along the highway to the turnoffs and parking lots. If you're looking to scuba dive or free dive, head for **Gerstle Cove,** accessible from the visitors center just south of Salt Point proper. The cove was designated one of California's first underwater parks, and divers who can deal with the chilly water have a wonderful time exploring the diverse undersea wildlife.

Kruse Rhododendron State Reserve

For a genteel experience, head east off Highway 1 to the **Kruse Rhododendron State Reserve** (Hwy. 1 near milepost 43, 707/847-3221, www.parks.ca.gov, daily sunrise-sunset, free), where you can meander along the **China Gulf Trail** in the spring, admiring the profusion of pink rhododendron flowers blooming beneath the second-growth redwood forest. If you prefer a picnic, you'll find tables at many of the beaches—just be aware that the North Coast can be quite windy in the summer.

Note that some facilities within this park have been closed due to the ongoing state budget crisis. Call 707/865-2391 before you go, or check the website to make sure the specific area you're headed to is open.

Stewart's Point

Stewart's Point is home to a post office, a small store, and a restaurant—and that's it. **Stewart's Point Store** (32000 S. Hwy. 1, 707/785-2406, www.stewartspoint.net, daily 6am-8pm, hours vary by season) sells groceries, wine, collectible dishes, hand-knitted hats, and Hostess Zingers. They've also got a deli and a bakery on-site. Upstairs, locally grown dinners are served in a historic dancehall (Fri.-Sat. 6:15pm, $10-32).

THE SEA RANCH

The last 10 miles of the Sonoma Coast before entering Mendocino County are the property of The Sea Ranch, a private coastal community. In the late 1960s, developers purchased a former sheep ranch, planning to build homes that blended into the natural environment. Development was met with opposition from environmental and coastal access groups, which led to the formation of the California Coastal Commission, a state agency that overlooks land use and coastal access on the state's coastline. Sea Ranch was eventually built, but the number of lots was reduced by half, and the development included six points for public access to the ocean, including Gualala Point Regional Park.

Today, the community is known for its distinctive buildings with wood sidings and shingles. One of its structures, Condominium 1, won the American Institute of Architects Gold Medal in 1991 and is now on the National Register of Historic Places. Those hard-fought coastal access points make the Sea Ranch a good place to take a break from driving for a short beach stroll. Visitors who want to linger in this low-key community can spend the night at The Sea Ranch Lodge.

◖ The Sea Ranch Chapel

Looking from the outside like a wooden stingray with a plume on top, The **Sea Ranch Chapel** (mile marker 55.66 Hwy. 1, on the right side of the highway, intersection of Hwy. 1 and Bosun's Reach, www.thesearanchchapel. org, daily sunrise-sunset) is one of the smallest and most creatively designed places of worship that you'll ever see. Designed by architect James Hubble, this tiny building's beautiful interior has polished redwood benches, three stained glass windows, a stone floor with an inserted mosaic, along with embedded local sea shells and sea urchins throughout the structure.

Annapolis Winery

You'll find a pleasant coastal climate and a small list of classic California wines at **Annapolis Winery** (26055 Soda Springs Rd., Annapolis, 707/886-5460, www.annapoliswinery.com, daily noon-5pm, tasting free), a small family-owned winery seven miles east of Sea Ranch. You can usually taste pinot,

the unique and very tiny Sea Ranch Chapel

cabernet, zinfandel, and port, depending on what they've made this year and what's in stock when you arrive. Take a glass outside to enjoy the views from the estate vineyards out over the forested mountains.

Sports and Recreation

With its front nine holes perched above the Pacific, the **Sea Ranch Golf Links** (42000 Hwy. 1, 707/785-2468, www.searanchgolf. com, Mon.-Thurs. $50, Fri.-Sun. and holidays $60) are like the legendary golf courses at Pebble Beach except without the crowds. Designed by Robert Muir Graves, the course also allows you to putt past redwood trees.

Accommodations and Food

Situated on 52 acres of prime coastal real estate, **Sea Ranch Lodge** (2.5 miles north of Stewart's Point on Hwy. 1, 707/785-2371, http://searanchlodge.com, $249-399) offers 19 rooms, all with simple 1960s throwback decor and ocean vistas that evoke paintings. Hiking trails on the grounds offer a self-guided wildflower walk and a short walk to Black Point Beach. Most rooms are equipped with gas fireplaces for those foggy days on the Sonoma Coast. The walls might be a bit thinner than more modern hotels so earplugs are provided. Guests are also treated to a fine complimentary hot breakfast at the lodge's **Black Point Grill** (2.5 miles north of Stewart's Point on Hwy. 1, 707/785-2371, daily 8am-11am, 11:30am-4:30pm, 5:30pm-9pm, $13-27). Black Point Grill is also open to the public, serving everything from burgers to local seafood in a dining area with large windows facing the sea.

Mendocino Coast

The Mendocino coast is a popular retreat for those who've been introduced to its specific charms. On weekends, Bay Area residents flock north to their favorite hideaways to enjoy windswept beaches, secret coves, and luscious cuisine. This area is ideal for deep-sea anglers, wine aficionados, and fans of luxury spas. Art is especially prominent in the culture; from the 1960s onward, aspiring artists have found supportive communities, sales opportunities, and homes in Mendocino County, and a number of small galleries display local artwork.

Be aware that the most popular inns fill up fast many weekends year-round. Fall-winter is the high season, with the Crab Festival, the Mushroom Festival, and various harvest and after-harvest wine celebrations. If you want to stay someplace specific on the Mendocino Coast, book your room at least a month in advance for weekday stays and six months or more in advance for major festival weekends.

GUALALA

With a population of 585, Gualala ("wa-LA-la") feels like a metropolis along the Highway 1 corridor in this region. While it's not the most charming coastal town, it does have some of the services other places lack.

Since 1961, the **Art in the Redwoods Festival** (46501 Gualala Rd., 707/884-1138, www.gualalaarts.org, mid-Aug., adults $6, under age 17 free) and its parent organization, Gualala Arts, have been going strong. This major event takes place over the course of a long weekend in mid-August and is run by the same people who bring you the Whale and Jazz Festival in Point Arena in April. Now featuring gallery exhibitions, special dinners, a champagne preview, bell ringers, a quilt raffle, and awards for the artists, this festival is a great reason to get the whole family to Gualala for some renewal and inspiration.

Accommodations

When it comes to food and lodging in Gualala,

you're not going to hear so many of those Sonoma and Mendocino County adjectives—"luxurious, elegant, pricey"—but you will find choices, which may be welcome.

For the budget-conscious, a good option is **The Surf Motel** (39170 Hwy. 1, 707/884-3571 or 888/451-7873, www.surfinngualala.com, $99-209). Only a few of the more expensive guest rooms have ocean views, but a full hot breakfast and wireless Internet access are included for all guests.

The **Breakers Inn** (39300 Hwy. 1, 707/884-3200, www.breakersinn.com, $185-245) has 28 uniquely decorated rooms named after states and countries. All have decks, spas, and fireplaces.

The **Whale Watch Inn** (35100 Hwy. 1, 800/942-5342, www.whalewatchinn.com, $190-280) specializes in romance. Each of its 18 individually decorated, luxuriously appointed guest rooms has an ocean view and a wood burning stove. Most also have whirlpool tubs. Every morning, a hot breakfast is delivered to your room.

Four miles north of Gualala, the **North Coast Country Inn** (34591 S. Hwy. 1, 707/884-4537, www.northcoastcountryinn.com, $195-225) was once part of a coastal sheep ranch. Six rooms are outfitted with antique furnishings and fireplaces; three also have kitchenettes. Mornings at the North Coast Country Inn begin with a hot breakfast buffet. An antique store and art gallery are also on the inn's grounds.

Camping

Two nearby parks provide good camping options. One is **Gualala River Redwood Park** (46001 Gualala Rd., 707/884-3533, www.gualalapark.com, May-Oct., day use $5 pp, camping $38-45 for 2 people); the other is **Gualala Point Regional Park** (42401 Hwy. 1, 707/785-2377, www.sonoma-county.org, day use $6 per vehicle, camping $28-32), one mile south of the town of Gualala, technically in

in tender, flavorful beef brisket, Memphis pulled pork, and St. Louis-style pork ribs.

Locals and visitors rave about the tacos at **Antonio's Tacos** (38820 S. Hwy. 1, 707/884-1789, Mon.-Sat. 8am-7pm, $2-12).

The Gualala **farmers market** (47950 Center St., www.mcfarm.org/gualala, late May-early Nov. Sat. 9:30am-12:30pm) is at the Gualala Community Center. **Surf** (39250 S. Hwy. 1, 707/884-4184, www.surfsuper.com, Sat.-Wed. 7:30am-7pm, Thurs.-Fri. 7:30am-8pm) is a supermarket that also sells flatbread pizzas and sandwiches.

Getting There and Around

Gualala is located 115 miles north of San Francisco on Highway 1, and 60 miles south of Fort Bragg. The **Mendocino Transit Authority** (707/462-1422 or 800/696-4682, www.4mta.org) has a bus line that connects Gualala to Fort Bragg.

POINT ARENA

A small coastal town located 1.5 miles south of its namesake point, Point Arena might be one of the North Coast's best secrets. The town's Main Street is Highway 1, which has a couple of bars, restaurants, markets, and the Arena Theater, which attracts all sorts of cultural events. One mile from the small downtown section is the scenic Point Arena Cove, which has a small fishing pier with rocky beaches on either side. The cove feels like the town's true center, a meeting place where fisherfolk constantly take in the conditions of the ocean. Just north and south of Point Arena on Highway 1 are some great coastal access points.

Sights
POINT ARENA LIGHTHOUSE

Although its magnificent Fresnel lens no longer turns through the night, the **Point Arena Lighthouse** (45500 Lighthouse Rd., 707/882-2777 or 877/725-4448, www.pointarena-lighthouse.com, summer daily 10am-4:30pm, winter daily 10am-3:30pm, adults $7.50, children $1) remains a Coast Guard light and fog station. But what makes this beacon special

Sonoma County. Both places offer redwoods, the ocean, and the river.

Food

Bones Roadhouse (39080 Hwy. 1, 707/884-1188, www.bonesroadhouse.com, restaurant Mon.-Fri. 11:30am-8 or 9pm, Sat.-Sun. 8am-8 or 9pm, bar 11:30am-10pm, $14-24) advertises its "BBQ, brews and blues." It delivers. This casual barbecue and beer joint at the north end of town cooks its meats on a wood-burning, custom-built smoker for 4-12 hours, which results

the Mendocino coast, north of Fort Bragg

is its history. When the 1906 earthquake hit San Francisco, it jolted the land all the way up the coast, severely damaging the Point Arena Lighthouse. When the structure was rebuilt two years later, engineers devised the aboveground foundation that gives the lighthouse both its distinctive shape and additional structural stability.

Visitors can enjoy the Lighthouse's extensive interpretive museum, which is housed in the fog station beyond the gift shop. Docentled tours up to the top of the lighthouse are well worth the trip, both for the views of the lighthouse from the top and for the fascinating story of its destruction and rebirth through the 1906 earthquake as told by the knowledgeable staff. Tour groups also have the opportunity to climb right up to the Fresnel lens, taking a rare close look at an astonishing invention that reflected pre-electric light far enough out to sea to protect passing ships. For those who just can't get enough of the lighthouse during daylight hours, consider staying in one of the four former lighthouse keepers' homes (877/725-4448, palight@mcn.org, $125-300, two-night minimum).

ARENA THEATER

If you prefer your entertainment on a screen but still like a little atmosphere, take in a show at the **Arena Theater** (214 Main St., 707/882-3456, www.arenatheater.org). This onetime vaudeville theater was also a movie palace of the old school when it opened in 1929. In the 1990s, the old theater got a restorative facelift that returned it to its art deco glory. Today, you can see all kinds of films at the Arena, from recent box office toppers to new documentaries and unusual independent films. If a film isn't playing, you might find a live musical or theatrical show.

MANCHESTER STATE PARK

Seven miles north of the town of Point Arena, **Manchester State Park** (44500 Kinney Lane, Manchester, 707/937-5804, day use free) is a wild place perfect for a long solitary beach walk. The 3.5-mile-long coast is littered with

the lonely coastline of Manchester State Park

bleached white driftwood and logs that lie on the dark sand like giant bones as waves crash. Even the water offshore is protected as part of the 3,782-acre Point Arena State Marine Reserve. At the southwestern tip of the park is Arena Rock, a nautical hazard known for sinking at least six ships before the construction of the nearby Point Arena Lighthouse to the south.

Part of the 1,500 acres of onshore parkland was once a dairy ranch. Now, there's beach, dunes, a wetlands trail, and a campground. The drive-in campground ($25, first come, first served) has 41 sites with basic amenities, including fire pits, picnic tables, and pit toilets. Some environmental campsites in the dunes are accessible via a one-mile hike in. The sounds of crashing waves nearby will lull you to sleep.

SCHOONER GULCH STATE BEACH
The area around Point Arena is filled with coastal access points. A local favorite is **Schooner Gulch State Beach** (intersection of Schooner Gulch Rd. and Hwy. 1, three miles south of the town of Point Arena, 707/937-5804, www.parks.ca.gov). From a pull-out north of Schooner Gulch Bridge, trails lead to two different beaches. The southern trail leads to **Schooner Gulch Beach,** a wide sandy expanse with rocky headlands and a stream flowing into the sea. But the northern trail leads to a more memorable destination: **Bowling Ball Beach.** At low tide, the ocean recedes to reveal small spherical boulders lined up in rows. Strike! (Unfortunately, the trail to Bowling Ball Beach is prone to closure due to erosion; you may want to call ahead to see if it is open.)

Entertainment and Events
215 Main (215 Main St., 707/882-3215, Mon.-Sat. 2:15pm-2am) is located at—guess where?—215 Main Street. This bar specializes in local wine and beer, with 40 bottles of wine and six beers on tap. There's a heated patio out back. Local dive bar **Sign of the Whale** (194 Main St., 707/882-2259, Mon.-Thurs. 4pm-10pm, Fri.-Sat. 4pm-midnight) is across the street.

© STUART THORNTON

scenic Point Arena Cove

The annual **Whale and Jazz Festival** (707/884-1138, www.gualalaarts.org/whale-jazz) takes place all around Mendocino County in April each year. Some of the nation's finest jazz performers play in a variety of venues, while the whales put on their own show out in the Pacific. Point Arena Lighthouse offers whale-watching from the shore each day, and the wineries and restaurants of the region provide refreshment and relaxation every evening of the festival weekend.

Accommodations

From 1901 to 1957, the ◖**Coast Guard House** (695 Arena Cove, 707/882-2442 or 800/524-9320, www.coastguardhouse.com, $165-265) was a working Coast Guard Life-Saving Station. Now the main building, which used to house the enlisted men, hosts overnight guests, who enjoy nice views of Point Arena Cove. Four rooms are available, including a suite with two bedrooms. Two detached cottages on-site offer more privacy. Restaurants are just a short walk away. The friendly and informative innkeepers serve a nice hot breakfast in the main house every morning.

Next door to the Coast Guard House is the **Wharf Master's Inn** (785 Iverson Ave., 707/882-3171 or 800/392-4031, www.wharf-masters.com, $105-550). Every room has a fireplace, a two-person spa, and a private deck. The Wharf Master's House has a kitchen and can accommodate up to eight people.

Food

Arena Market & Café (183 Main St., 707/882-3663, www.arenaorganics.org, summer Mon.-Sat. 7am-7pm, Sun. 8am-6pm, winter Mon.-Fri. 7am-6pm, Sat. 7am-5pm, Sun. 8am-5pm) is a co-op committed to a philosophy of local, sustainable, and organic food, and they do their best to compensate farmers fairly and keep money in the community. This is a medium-size grocery store, so you can stock up on staples or sit at one of the tables in the front of the store and enjoy a bowl of homemade soup or coffee. They're one of the only places in town with Wi-Fi.

The **Uneda Eat Café** (206 Main St., 707/882-3800, www.pangaeacatering.com, Thurs.-Sat. 5pm-8pm, $12-22) preserves the sign of the former owner, who was an Italian butcher: The storefront still says "Uneda Meat Market." Now a dine-in, take-out, and catering operation run by Jill and Rob Hunter, who previously owned the popular Pangaea Restaurant, the menu is decidedly locavore.

Blue on the outside, pink on the inside, **Franny's Cup and Saucer** (213 Main St., 707/882-2500, www.frannyscupandsaucer.com, Wed.-Sat. 8am-4pm) is whimsical and welcoming. The owners, Franny and her mother, Barbara, do all their own baking and they even make truffles and other candies from scratch. It's takeout only, so stop in and pick up a picnic before you go to the lighthouse or one of the parks.

Slightly north of town is **Rollerville Café** (22900 S. Hwy. 1, 707/882-2077, www.rollervillecafe.com, Mon.-Thurs. and Sun. 8am-2pm, Fri.-Sat. 8am-7:30pm, lunch $8-10, dinner $20-24). Dinner may seem a little pricey, but lunch is available all day; breakfast is 8am-11am. This is a small homey place catering to guests at the adjacent timeshare resort as well as locals and travelers.

On the second floor of a two-story building, the **Pier Chowder House & Tap Room** (790 Port Rd., 707/882-3400, www.thepierchowderhouse.com, daily 11am-9pm, $18-25) has an outside deck perfect for taking in the sunset over Point Arena's scenic cove. The menu focuses on seafood. Go for the salmon or rock cod in season; both are caught by local anglers. There is also a long bar with 26 beers on tap.

In the same building as the Pier Chowder House, **Cove Coffee and Tackle** (790 Port Rd., 707/882-2665, $5.50) attracts locals with tasty items like "Nate's Special," an egg sandwich with pesto, cream cheese, sausage, onion, and Swiss cheese. It's a perfect place to go for a morning coffee.

The weekly **Mendocino County Farmer's Market** (214 Main St., 707/964-6718, www.mcfarm.org, Wed. 10:30am-1pm) is in the Point Arena Theater parking lot.

Information and Services

The **Coast Community Library** (225 Main St., 707/882-3114, www.coastcommunitylibrary.org, Mon. and Fri. noon-6pm, Tues. 10am-6pm, Wed. 10am-8pm, Thurs. noon-8pm, Sat. noon-3pm) is a real hub of activity thanks to its central location—the impressive 1928 Point Arena Mercantile Company building—and its free Internet access.

Getting There and Around

Point Arena is located 10 miles north of Gualala on Highway 1, and about 120 miles north of San Francisco.

The **Mendocino Transit Authority** (800/696-4682, www.4mta.org) runs the route 75 bus to connect Point Arena south to Gualala and north to Fort Bragg. The bus usually runs once a day, although schedules are subject to change; contact the transit authority for details.

ELK

The town of Elk used to be called Greenwood, after the family of Caleb Greenwood, who settled here in about 1850. Details of the story vary, but it is widely believed that Caleb was part of a mission to rescue survivors of the Donner Party after their rough winter near Truckee.

Greenwood State Beach

From the mid-19th century until the 1920s, the stretch of shore at **Greenwood State Beach** (Hwy. 1, 707/937-5804, www.parks.ca.gov, visitors center mid-March-Oct. Sat.-Sun. 11am-1pm) was a stop for large ships carrying timber to points of sale in San Francisco and sometimes even China. The visitors center displays photographs and exhibits about Elk's past in the lumber business. It also casts light on the Native American heritage of the area and the natural resources that are still abundant.

A short hike demonstrates what makes this area so special. From the parking lot, follow the trail down toward the ocean. You'll soon come to a fork; to the right is a picnic area. Follow the left fork to another picnic site and then, soon afterward, the beach. Turn left and walk about

© STUART THORNTON

the view from Elk Cove Inn

0.25 miles to reach Greenwood Creek. Shortly past it is a cliff, at which point you have to turn around and walk back up the hill. Even in the short amount of time it takes to do this walk, you'll experience lush woods, sandy cliffs, and dramatic ocean overlooks. In winter, the walk can be dark and blustery and even more intriguing, although it's a pleasure in any season.

Greenwood State Beach is alongside the town of Elk, 10-15 miles north of Point Arena and about 17 miles south of Mendocino.

Accommodations and Food

Perched on a hillside over the stunning Greenwood State Beach cove, the **◖ Elk Cove Inn** (6300 S. Hwy. 1, 800/275-2967, www. elkcoveinn.com, $135-395) offers luxury accommodations, generous hospitality, and superb views of the nearby Pacific, studded with islands and a scattering of offshore rocks. Check-in comes with a complimentary glass of wine or cocktail and a welcome basket filled with goodies including fresh baked cookies. Choose from reasonably priced rooms in the

main house, cozy cabins with an ocean view, or luxurious suites with jetted soaking tubs and private balconies or patios. A private staircase leads down to the beach below, where you can build a campfire or stroll the uncrowded coastline. There's also a full service day spa with a sauna and aromatherapy steam shower. The innkeepers have thought of everything to make your stay top notch, from port wine and chocolates in the rooms to the big morning breakfast buffet of Southern comfort food.

Elk is also home to the luxurious **Griffin House Inn** (5910 S. Hwy. 1, 707/877-3422, www.griffinn.com, $145-325), which offers lovely cottages with oceanfront decks. The lack of TVs and phones in the rooms ensures peace and quiet. Full breakfast can be delivered to your guest room, but there's also a lively dining room.

Housed in a little blue cottage attached to the Griffin House Inn, **Bridget Dolan's Pub & Restaurant** (5910 S. Hwy. 1, 707/877-1820, www.griffinn.com) is a terrific place to hole up with a draft beer on a rainy winter day or fog-laden summer afternoon. The tables are draped in white tablecloths and the small bar is lined with locals. The menu includes burgers, pizzas, and hearty pub fare like cottage pie.

With a perfect location in the center of town and across the street from the ocean, **Queenie's Roadhouse Café** (6061 Hwy. 1, Thurs.-Mon. 8am-3pm, $7-16) is the place to go for hot food and a friendly atmosphere.

The **Beacon Light by the Sea** (7401 S. Hwy. 1, south of Elk, 707/877-3311, Fri.-Sat. 5pm-11pm) is the best bar in the area. Its colorful owner, R. D. Beacon, was born in Elk and has run the Beacon Light since 1971. He claims it's the only place you can get hard liquor for 14 miles in any direction. With 54 different brands of vodka, 20 whiskeys, and 15 tequilas, there's something for every sort of drinker. On clear days, the views stretch all the way to the Point Arena Lighthouse.

ALBION AND LITTLE RIVER

Tiny Albion is along Highway 1 almost 30 miles north of Point Arena and about 8 miles south of Mendocino. Little River is about five miles farther north, also on Highway 1. There is a **post office** (7748 Hwy. 1, Albion, 707/937-5547, www.usps.com, Mon.-Fri. 8:15am-1pm and 2pm-4:30pm), a state park, and several plush places to stay.

Van Damme State Park

The centerpiece of **Van Damme State Park** (Hwy. 1, 3 miles south of Mendocino, 707/937-5804, www.parks.ca.gov, daily 8am-9pm, free) is the **Pygmy Forest,** where you'll see a true biological rarity: Mature yet tiny cypress and pine trees perpetually stunted by a combination of always-wet ground and poor soil-nutrient conditions. To get there, drive along Airport Road to the trail parking lot (opposite the county airport) and follow the wheelchair-accessible loop trail (0.25 miles, easy). You can also get there by hiking along the **Fern Canyon Trail** (7 miles round-trip, difficult).

Kayak Mendocino (707/937-0700, www.kayakmendocino.com, board surfing $30 per hour) launches four Sea Cave Nature Tours (9am, 11:30am, 2pm, and sunset, $50 pp) from Van Damme State Park. No previous experience is necessary; the expert guides provide all the equipment you need and teach you how to paddle your way through the sea caves and around the harbor seals.

Accommodations

Tired of typical cookie cutter motel rooms? There's no place quite like **The Andiron** (6051 N. Hwy. 1, Little River, 707/937-1543, www.theandiron.com, $109-259). The one- and two-room cabins in a meadow above Highway 1 are filled with curiosities and intentional kitsch. Every room is different. One has a one-of-a-kind camel-shaped bar, while another has a coin-operated vibrating bed. Most have vintage board games, View-Masters, and an eclectic library of books. Standard amenities include small wooden decks and small flat screen TVs. A hot tub under the trees is available for guests. The fun-loving owners throw happy hour parties every weekend, including "Fondue Fridays," when they serve the melted

cheese dish along with local beers and wines. The Andiron isn't fancy, but it sure is fun.

The **Albion River Inn** (3790 N. Hwy. 1, 6 miles south of Mendocino, 707/937-1919 or 800/479-7944, www.albionriverinn.com, $195-325) is a gorgeous and serene setting for an away-from-it-all vacation. A full breakfast is included in the room rates, but pets and smoking are not allowed, and there are no TVs.

The **Little River Inn** (7901 N. Hwy. 1, Little River, 707/937-5942 or 888/466-5683, www.littleriverinn.com, $130-375) appeals to coastal vacationers who like a little luxury. It has a nine-hole golf course and two lighted tennis courts, and all its recreation areas overlook the Pacific, which crashes on the shore just across the highway from the inn. The sprawling white Victorian house and barns hide the sprawl of the grounds, which also have a great restaurant and a charming sea-themed bar. Relax even more at the in-house Spa at Little River Inn.

Stevenswood Spa Resort (8211 N. Hwy. 1, Little River, 800/421-2810, www.stevenswood.com, $269-499) is a modern facility with contemporary decor. A classy restaurant and a day spa help you feel relaxed and pampered, as does Van Damme State Park, which surrounds the resort on three sides. Be sure to book one of the outdoor in-ground hot tubs at the spa for a relaxing evening.

Camping

There's camping on the coast at **Van Damme State Park** (Hwy. 1, 707/937-5804, www.parks.ca.gov, reservations 800/444-7275, www.reserveamerica.com, $35), three miles south of Mendocino. The appealing campground offers picnic tables, fire rings, and food lockers, as well as restrooms and hot showers. The park's 1,831 acres include beaches as well as forest, so there's lots of natural beauty to enjoy. Reservations are strongly encouraged.

Food

Ledford House Restaurant (3000 N. Hwy. 1, Albion, 707/937-0282, www.ledfordhouse.com, Wed.-Sun. 5pm-close, $19-30) is beautiful even from a distance; you'll see it on the hill as you drive up Highway 1. With excellent food and nightly jazz performances, it's one of the truly "special occasion" choices in the area.

Tucked into a corner of a convenience store, the **Little River Market Grill & Gourmet Deli** (7746 N. Hwy. 1, Little River, 707/937-5133, Mon.-Fri. 8:30am-6:30pm, Sat.-Sun. 8:30am-7:30pm, $8) is a local's favorite. This better-than-average deli has a surprisingly wide range of options, including burgers, pulled pork sandwiches, and fish tacos. Nice vegetarian options include the tasty pesto veggie and avocado sandwich. This is the place to grab a sandwich for a picnic on the Mendocino Coast.

Stevenswood Spa Resort has a fine on-site restaurant, **The Restaurant at Stevenswood** (8211 N. Hwy. 1, Little River, 707/937-2810, www.stevenswood.com, Thurs.-Tues. 5:30pm-9pm, $22-28).

◖ MENDOCINO

Perched on a headlands surrounded by the Pacific, Mendocino is one of the most picturesque towns on the California coast. Quaint bed-and-breakfasts, art colonies, and local sustainable dining add to its charm, making it a favorite for romantic weekend getaways.

Once a logging town, Mendocino was reborn as an artist community in the 1950s. One of its most striking buildings is the town's Masonic Hall, dating from 1866 and adorned with a redwood statue of Father Time on its roof. Many New Englanders settled in the region in its early years. With its old water towers and historic buildings, it resembles a New England fishing village—so much that it played one in the long-running TV series *Murder, She Wrote.* It was also a stand-in for Monterey in the 1955 James Dean film *East of Eden.*

Mendocino Art Center

The town of Mendocino has long been an inspiration and a gathering place for artists of many varieties, and the **Mendocino Art Center** (45200 Little Lake St., 707/937-5818 or 800/653-3328, www.mendocinoartcenter. org, daily 10am-5pm, donation) is the main institution that gives these diverse artists a community, provides them with opportunities for teaching and learning, and displays the work of contemporary artists for the benefit of both the artists and the general public. Since 1959 the center has offered artist workshops and retreats. Today it has a flourishing schedule of events and classes, five galleries, and a sculpture garden. You can even drop in and make some art of your own. Supervised "open studios" in ceramics, jewelry making, watercolor, sculpture, and drawing take place throughout the year (call for specific schedules, $7-10 per session).

Kelley House Museum

The mission of the lovely, stately **Kelley House Museum** (45007 Albion St., 707/937-5791, www.kelleyhousemuseum.org, summer Thurs.-Tues. 11am-3pm, Oct.-May Fri.-Mon. 11am-3pm, free, tours Sat. 11am, $2) is to preserve the history of Mendocino for future generations. The new addition to the historic house is home to the village archives, which include thousands of photos. In the museum, antique furniture and fixtures grace the rooms. A collection of Victorian clothing, photos, and documents illuminate the story of historic Mendocino, and knowledgeable docents are available to offer more information. Ask about the town's water-rights issues for a great lesson in the untold history of the Mendocino Coast. On weekends, docents lead two-hour walking tours ($10) that detail Mendocino's history.

Mendocino Headlands State Park

No trip to Mendocino is complete without a walk along the rugged coastline of **Mendocino Headlands State Park** (west of town, 707/937-5804, www.parks.ca.gov, daily sunrise-sunset). A series of trails along the seaside cliffs west of town offer views of the area's sea caves and coves. It's a favorite spot for painters and photographers hoping to capture the majesty of the coast. In winter, the park is a great vantage point for viewing migrating gray whales. In town, the **Historic Ford House** (735 Main St., 707/937-5397, www.mendoparks.org, daily 11am-4pm, free, donations encouraged)

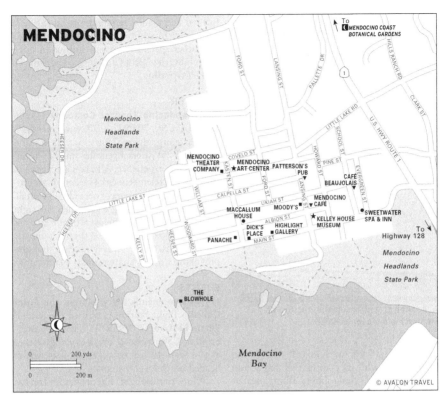

doubles as the Mendocino Headlands State Park Visitor Center.

Point Cabrillo Light Station

Whether you're into scenery or history, nautical or otherwise, you won't want to miss a visit to the **Point Cabrillo Light Station Historic Park** (45300 Lighthouse Rd., 707/937-6122, www.pointcabrillo.org, daily 11am-4pm, $5), north of Mendocino and south of Caspar and Fort Bragg. This beautiful lighthouse has been functioning for more than 100 years since it was built, in part to facilitate the movement of lumber and other supplies south to San Francisco to help rebuild the city after the massive 1906 earthquake. The light station was absorbed into the California State Park system in 2002, and in 2009 became a victim of state budget cuts and saw its services curtailed. The

site is currently being managed by a volunteer organization, the Point Cabrillo Lightkeepers Association. You can take a tour of the famous Fresnel lens, learn about the infamous *Frolic* shipwreck of 1850, and explore the tide-pool aquarium. If you don't want to leave the light station grounds after sundown, consider renting the light keeper's house or two cottages on the grounds for an evening (707/937-5033, www.mendocinovacations.com).

Entertainment and Events
BARS

For a place to hunker down over a pint in Mendocino, head to cozy **Patterson's Pub** (10485 Lansing St., 707/937-4782, www.pattersonspub.com, bar daily 10am-midnight, restaurant daily 11am-11pm). This traditional Irish-style pub is in the former rectory of a

A wooden statue resides on the top of Mendocino's Masonic Hall.

STUART THORNTON

19th-century Catholic church. It nods to the 21st century with six plasma TVs that screen current games. Order a simple, filling meal at the tables or at the bar, where you'll find 14 beers on tap, a full-fledged wine list, and hard liquor imported from around the world.

So where do the locals go for a drink in heavily visited Mendocino? That would be **Dick's Place** (45080 Main St., 707/937-6010, daily 11:30am-2am), sometimes called Richard's by the Sea. Dick's is an old school, cash-only bar, with a mounted buck head draped in Christmas lights as decor. Dick's is easy to find: Look for the only neon sign on Main Street, in the shape of a martini glass.

LIVE MUSIC

For live music on the Mendocino coast, head to the **Caspar Inn** (14957 Caspar Rd., Caspar, 707/964-5565, www.casparinn.com, Tues.-Sat. 5pm-2am, Sun. 5pm-midnight, cover varies), about five miles north of Mendocino and six miles south of Fort Bragg. The Caspar offers a full bar and a good restaurant menu ($10-22, cash only) in addition to its lineup of bands and other special events, including an open mic night, the "Pool Challenge," and "micro-midget wrestling."

THEATER

The **Mendocino Theater Company** (45200 Little Lake St., 707/937-4477, www.mendocinotheatre.org, shows Thurs.-Sat. 8pm, Sun. 2pm, $10-25) offers a genuine small community-theater experience. All plays are staged in the 81-seat Helen Schoeni Theater for an intimate night of live drama or comedy. The small, old weathered building exudes just the right kind of charm to draw in lovers of quirky community theater. But this little theater company has big goals, and it tends to take on thought-provoking work by contemporary playwrights.

EVENTS

For two weekends every March, the Point Cabrillo Light Station is host to the annual **Whale Festival** (707/937-6123, www.pointcabrillo.org, $5), a chance to get expert guidance as you scan the sea for migrating gray whales headed north for the summer.

In July, musicians of all types descend on the temporarily warmish coast for the **Mendocino Music Festival** (707/937-2044, www.mendocinomusic.com, concert ticket prices vary). For 2.5 weeks, live performances are held at venues around the area. There's always chamber music, orchestral concerts, opera, jazz, and bluegrass, and there's usually world music, blues, singer-songwriters, and dance performances. A centerpiece of the festival is the famed big-band concert. In addition to 13 evenings of music, there are three series of daytime concerts: piano, jazz, and village chamber concerts. No series passes are available; all events require separate tickets.

If restaurants are the heart of the Mendocino food scene, festivals are its soul. **Taste of Mendocino** (http://winecrab.com) comprises a couple of sub festivals: **Mendocino Crab & Wine Days** takes place in January and offers a burst of crab-related events (prices vary);

Mendocino's Point Cabrillo Light Station

in November, the focus is on the wild mushroom season, and you can come to the **Wine & Mushroom Festival** for classes, tastings, and tours (prices vary) to learn to cook or just to eat. Check the website for a plethora of other special events.

Shopping

On the coast, the best place to browse is **Mendocino Village.** Not only are the galleries and boutiques welcoming and fun, the whole downtown area is beautiful. It seems that every shop in the Main Street area has its own garden, and each fills with a riotous cascade of flowers in the summer. Even if you hate to shop, make the trip down to the village just to literally smell the roses.

Panache (45120 Main St., 707/937-0947, www.thepanachegallery.com, daily 10:30am-5pm) displays and sells beautiful works of art in all sorts of media. You'll find paintings, jewelry, sculpture, and art glass. Much of the artistic focus is reminiscent of the sea crashing just outside the large multiple-room gallery.

The wooden furniture and boxes are a special treat: handmade treasures using rare woods are combined and then sanded and polished to silk-smooth finishes.

If you love fine woodworking and hand-crafted furniture, you will not want to miss the **Highlight Gallery** (45052 Main St., 707/937-3132, www.thehighlightgallery.com, daily 10am-5pm). Although the gallery has branched out in recent years to feature glasswork, ceramics, painting, and sculpture, its roots are in woodwork, which it maintains as a focus.

Sports and Recreation

HIKING

Some of the most popular hiking trails in coastal Mendocino wind through **Russian Gulch State Park** (Hwy. 1, 2 miles north of Mendocino, 707/937-5804, www.parks.ca.gov, $8). Russian Gulch has its own **Fern Canyon Trail** (3 miles round-trip), winding into the second-growth redwood forest filled with lush green ferns. At the four-way junction, turn left to hike another 0.75 miles to the ever-popular waterfall. Be aware that you're likely to be part of a crowd visiting the falls on summer weekends. To the right at the four-way junction you can take a three-mile loop for a total hike of six miles that leads to the top of the attractive little waterfall. If you prefer the shore to the forest, hike west rather than east to take in the lovely wild headlands and see blowholes, grasses, and even trawlers out seeking the day's catch. The biggest attraction is the **Devil's Punchbowl,** a collapsed sea cave 100 feet across and 60 feet deep. There's also a nice beach.

KAYAKING

Kayak and canoe trips are a popular summer activity on the Mendocino Coast. To explore the relatively sedate waters of the Big River estuary, consider renting an outrigger or even a sailing canoe from **Catch a Canoe & Bicycles Too** (44850 Comptche Ukiah Rd., 707/937-0273, www.catchacanoe.com, daily 9am-5pm, boat and bike rentals adults $28 pp for 1-3 hours, ages 6-17 $14 pp; guided tours June-Sept., $65 pp) at the Stanford Inn. The guided tours include an estuary excursion with a naturalist and a ride on an outrigger that utilizes solar energy for power.

SURFING

Big River is a beach break surf spot just south of the town of Mendocino where the Big River flows into the ocean. It's a spot you can check out from Highway 1, and on most days, all levels of surfers can try their hand at surfing the break. More experienced surfers should try **Smuggler's Cove,** located in Mendocino Bay on the south side of Big River. It's a reef break that usually just works during winter swells.

DIVING

A good spot for abalone is **The Blowhole** (end of Main St.), a favorite summer lounging spot for locals. In the water, you'll find abalone and their empty shells; colorful, tiny nudibranchs; and occasionally, overly friendly seals. The kelp beds just off the shore attract divers who don't fear cold water and want to check out the complex ecosystem. Check with the state

© STUART THORNTON

Russian Gulch State Park

Department of Fish and Game (888/773-8450, www.dfg.ca.gov) for the rules about taking abalone, which is strictly regulated; most species are endangered and can't be harvested. Game wardens can explain the abalone season opening and closing dates, catch limits, licensing information, and the best spots to dive each year.

SPAS

Of all the reasons people choose to vacation on the Mendocino Coast, the main one seems to be plain old relaxation. The perfect way to do so is to seek out one of the many nearby spas. The **Sweetwater Spa & Inn** (44840 Main St., 800/300-4140, www.sweetwaterspa.com, Sun.-Fri. noon-9pm, Sat. noon-10pm, $15-19/half-hour, $18-23/hour) rents indoor hot tubs by the half-hour and hour. They also have group tub and sauna rates ($10-20). Sweetwater offers a range of massage services ($90-154) at reasonable rates. The rustic buildings and garden setting complete the experience. Appointments are required for massage and private tubs, but walk-ins are welcome to use the communal tub and sauna.

For a massage in the comfort of your own accommodations, make an appointment for a foot rub, herbal facial, full-body massage, or acupuncture with **The Body Works** (707/357-5162, www.massagetime.biz, $125 per hour).

Accommodations
$150-250

The warm and welcoming **《 Blackberry Inn** (44951 Larkin Rd., 800/950-7806, www.blackberryinn.biz, $125-225) is in the hills, slightly out of the center of Mendocino. You may be a little confused when you first pull in, since it looks as though you're in a town—a perfectly stylized one from the Old West but without the shooting and the bank robberies. Each of the 16 guest rooms has a different storefront outside, including the bank, the saloon, the barbershop, and the land-grant office. Each is charmingly decorated and beautifully maintained with plush, comfortable bedding cozied up with colonial-style quilts, along with the modern convenience of microwaves, fridges, and free

wireless Internet. The manager-hosts are the nicest you'll find anywhere, and you check in at an office designed to resemble a train station.

《 Sweetwater Inn and Spa (44840 Main St., 800/300-4140, www.sweetwaterspa.com, $100-295) harks back to the days when Mendocino was a colony of starving artists rather than a weekend retreat for city dwellers. A redwood water tower was converted into a guest room, joined by a motley connection of detached cottages that guarantee guests great privacy. Every guest room and cottage has its own style—you'll find a spiral staircase in one of the water towers, a two-person tub set in a windowed alcove in the Zen Room, and fireplaces in many of the cottages. The eclectic decor makes each room different, and many return guests request their favorite guest room again. Thick gardens surround the building complex and a path leads back to the Garden Spa. The location, just past downtown on Main Street, is perfect for dining, shopping, and art walks.

The luxurious **Glendeven Inn** (8205 N. Hwy. 1, 707/937-0083 or 800/822-4536, www.glendeven.com, $175-295) is situated in a historic farmhouse with ocean views. The hosts will help you settle in with complimentary wine and hors d'oeuvres in the late afternoon, and wake you in the morning with a three-course made-to-order breakfast, delivered to your room. If you like the food (you will), consider joining them for a five-course **"farm-to-table" dinner** (Wed.-Thurs. and Sat. 6pm, by reservation only, dinner $65, with wine pairings $90).

The **Blue Door Inn** (10481 Howard St., 707/937-4892, www.bluedoorinn.com, $175-275) aims to spoil you. Five sleek, modern rooms come with flat screen TVs and gas fireplaces. The two-course breakfast features homemade pastries and egg dishes.

OVER $250

Up and away from the beaches, sitting amid redwoods, the **Stanford Inn** (44850 Comptche Ukiah Rd., 0.5 miles east of Hwy. 1, 707/937-5615 or 800/331-8884, www.stanfordinn.com, $211-555) is an upscale forest lodge. The location is convenient to hiking and only a short drive down to Mendocino Village and the coast. Guest rooms have beautiful, honey wood-paneled walls, pretty furniture, and puffy down comforters. If you're traveling with a group, consider one of the elegant two-bedroom suites, but be aware that "executive suite" means a junior suite. Other amenities include a wood-burning fireplace, a TV with a DVD player, Internet access, a stereo, a pool, sauna and hot tub, and free use of mountain bikes. Gardens surrounding the resort are perfect for strolling.

The 1882 **MacCallum House** (45020 Albion St., 707/936-0289 or 800/609-0492, www.maccallumhouse.com, $250-400) is the king of luxury on the Mendocino Coast. The facility includes several properties in addition to the main building in Mendocino Village. Choose from private cottages with hot tubs, suites with jetted tubs, and guest rooms with opulent antique appointments. The woodwork gleams and the service pleases. Note that there's a two-night minimum on weekends, and a three-night minimum for most holidays. Room rates include a cooked-to-order breakfast and a $14-per-room credit toward dinner.

The beautifully restored 1909 **Point Cabrillo Head Lightkeeper's House** (45300 Lighthouse Rd., 707/937-5033, www.mendocinovacations.com, 2-night minimum, $833-1,030 for 2 nights) is the home-away-from-home that you'll want to write home about. It's located atop a cliff beside the Pacific, so you can watch for whales, dolphins, and seabirds without leaving the porch. Four bedrooms sleep eight people, with 4.5 baths and a very modern kitchen. Larger groups such as family reunions or wedding parties can also rent two of the cottages nearby.

Food
CONTEMPORARY
One of the most appealing and dependable places to get a good meal any day of the week is the **Mendocino Café** (10451 Lansing St., 707/937-6141, www.mendocinocafe.com, daily 11am-4pm and 5pm-9pm, $14-32). The café

has good, simple, well-prepared food, a small kids menu, a wine list, and a beer list. Enjoy a Thai burrito, a fresh salmon fillet, or a steak in the warm, well-lit dining room. Or sit outside: The café is in the gardens of Mendocino Village, and thanks to a heated patio, you can enjoy outdoor dining any time of day.

FARMER'S MARKET
Mendocino has a weekly **Farmer's Market** (Howard St. and Main St., www.mcfarm.org, May-Oct. Fri. noon-2pm), where you can find seasonal produce, flowers, fish, wine, honey, and more.

FRENCH
¢ Café Beaujolais (961 Ukiah St., 707/937-5614, www.cafebeaujolais.com, lunch Wed.-Sun. 11:30am-2:30pm, dinner daily from 5:30pm, $23-35) is a standout French-California restaurant in an area dense with great upscale cuisine. This charming out-of-the-way spot is a few blocks from the center of Mendocino Village in an older creeper-covered home. Despite the white tablecloths and fancy crystal, the atmosphere is casual at lunchtime and gets only slightly more formal at dinner. The giant salads and delectable entrées are made with organic produce, humanely raised meats, and locally caught seafood. Beware: The portions can be enormous, but you can get them half-size just by asking. Having trouble deciding what to order? Ask the waitstaff, who are friendly, helpful, and quite knowledgeable about the menu and wine list—and the attractions of the local area, for that matter. Reservations are available on the website.

VEGETARIAN
Vegetarians and carnivores alike rave about **Ravens Restaurant** (Stanford Inn, 44850 Comptche Ukiah Rd., 0.5 miles east of Hwy. 1, 707/937-5615 or 800/331-8884, www.ravensrestaurant.com, Mon.-Sat. 8am-10:30am and 5:30pm-close, Sun. 8am-noon and 5:30pm-close, $18-23). Inside the lodge, which is surrounded by lush organic gardens, you'll find a big open dining room. Many of the vegetarian

and vegan dishes served use produce from the inn's own organic farm. At breakfast, enjoy delectable vegetarian (or vegan, with tofu) scrambles, omelets, and Florentines, complete with homemade breads and English muffins. At dinner, try one of the unusual salads or a seasonal vegetarian entrée. Even the wine list reflects organic, biodynamic, and sustainable-practice wineries.

Information and Services

Mendocino Village has a **post office** (10500 Ford St., 707/937-5282, www.usps.com, Mon.-Fri. 7:30am-4:30pm). **Moody's Internet Café, Art Gallery, and Coffee Bar** (10450 Lansing St., 707/937-4843, www.moodyscoffeebar. com, daily 6am-8pm) charges $2 per day for wireless Internet access if you bring your own laptop, and an hourly rate ($6) to use its computers.

Getting There and Around

It's simplest to navigate to and within Mendocino with your own vehicle. From U.S. 101 near Cloverdale, take Highway 128 northwest for 60 miles. Highway 128 becomes Highway 1 on the coast; Mendocino is another 10 miles north. A slower, more scenic alternative is to take Highway 1 the whole way from San Francisco to Mendocino; this route takes at least 4.5 hours. Mendocino has a fairly compact downtown area, Mendocino Village, with a concentration of restaurants, shops, and inns just a few blocks from the beach.

The **Mendocino Transit Authority** (800/696-4682, www.4mta.org) operates a dozen bus routes that connect Mendocino and Fort Bragg with larger cities like Santa Rosa and Ukiah, where you can make connections to Amtrak, Greyhound, and airports for access to farther-away points.

FORT BRAGG

A former military outpost and the home to a major logging company, Fort Bragg is the Mendocino Coast's largest city. With chain fast food joints and hotels lining Highway 1 as it passes through town, it doesn't have the immediate charm of its neighbor to the south. But it does offer some great restaurants, interesting downtown shops, and proximity to coastal landmarks, including Glass Beach and MacKerricher State Park.

Skunk Train

One of the famed attractions in Mendocino County is the California Western Railroad, popularly called the **Skunk Train** (depot at end of Laurel St., 866/457-5865, www.skunktrain. com, office winter daily 9am-2pm, summer daily 9am-3pm, adults $49, children $24), perfect for rail buffs and traveling families. The restored steam locomotives pull trains from the coast at Fort Bragg 40 miles through the redwood forest to the town of Willits and back. The adventure lets passengers see the true majesty of the redwoods while giving a hint about life in Northern California before the era of highways. The brightly-painted trains appeal to children, and the historic aspects and scenery call to adults. You can board in either Fort Bragg or Willits, making a round-trip to return to your lodgings for the night. Check the website for rides featuring beer and bratwurst or special events like a Halloween pumpkin patch excursion.

MacKerricher State Park

Three miles north of Fort Bragg, **MacKerricher State Park** (Hwy. 1, 707/964-9112, district office 707/937-5804, www.parks.ca.gov, daily sunrise-10pm, day use free) offers the small duck-filled Cleone Lake, six miles of sandy ocean beaches, four miles of cliffs and crags, and **camping** (reservations 800/444-7275, www.reserveamerica.com, $35). The main attraction for some is a gigantic, almost complete skeleton of a whale near the park entrance. Because there's no day use fee, you can stop in to see the whale even if you don't have time to hang out at the park. If you're lucky, you can also spot live whales and harbor seals frolicking in the ocean. The coast can be rough here, so don't swim or even wade unless it's what the locals call a "flat day"—no big waves and undertow. If the kids want to play in the water, take them to **Pudding Creek Beach** in the park, about 2.5 miles south of the campground, where they can play in the relatively sheltered area under the trestle bridge. Hikers will enjoy the **Ten Mile Beach Trail** (10 miles round-trip), actually an old logging road that goes from Laguna Point to Ten Mile River.

Glass Beach

The most famous beach in the Mendocino area, **Glass Beach** (Elm St. and Glass Beach Dr.) is not a miracle of nature. The unpleasant origin of this fascinating beach strewn with sea glass was the Fort Bragg city dump. As the ocean rose over the landfill, the heavy glass that had been dumped there stayed put. Years of pounding surf polished and smoothed the broken edges, and now the surf returns our human refuse to the shore. At the tideline, amber, green, and clear sea glass color the shore.

Beachcombers used to collect the smooth coated shards of glass; now that the beach is under the management of MacKerricher State Park, it's against the rules to remove them. But it's still quite a sight. The trail down to Glass Beach is short but steep and treacherous; don't wear sandals—good walking or hiking shoes and attention to safety are a must.

Triangle Tattoo Museum

This is not your grandmother's art museum, so enter at your own risk. For more than 20 years, the **Triangle Tattoo Museum** (356B N. Main St., 707/964-8814, www.triangletattoo.com, daily noon-6pm, free) has displayed the implements of tattooing and photos of their results. To enter, walk up a flight of narrow stairs and stare at the walls, which are completely covered with photos of tattoos. All forms of the art are represented, from those done by indigenous people to those done at carnivals and in prisons. In glass cases upstairs are all types of tattooing devices, some antique. More photos grace the walls of the warren of small rooms in a never-ending collage. The street-side rooms house a working tattoo parlor, and you can find intrepid artists and their canvases working late into the evening. If you're interested, talk to an artist about scheduling an appointment.

Lost Coast Culture Machine

Devotees of contemporary art will want to make a pilgrimage to the **Lost Coast Culture Machine** (190 E. Elm St., 707/961-1600, www.lostcoastculturemachine.org, Wed.-Sun. noon-5pm, donation). Calling itself an "artist-run contemporary art space and handmade paper mill," the venue's exhibitions, presentations, demonstrations, and events vary widely. There's always something interesting going on, and visitors are welcome to drop in.

Pacific Star Winery

The only winery on the Mendocino Coast, **Pacific Star Winery** (33000 N. Hwy. 1, 707/964-1155, www.pacificstarwinery.com, daily 11am-5pm, tasting free) makes the most of its location. Barrels of wine are left out in the salt air to age, incorporating a hint of the Pacific into each vintage. Friendly tasting-room staffers will tell you how much they like their bosses, the winemaker, and which of the winery cats most likes to be picked up. Wines are tasty and reasonably priced, and you can bring your own picnic to enjoy on the nearby bluff, which overlooks the ocean.

Mendocino Coast Botanical Gardens

Stretching 47 acres down to the sea, **Mendocino Coast Botanical Gardens** (18220 N. Hwy. 1, 707/964-4352, www.gardenbythesea.org, Mar.-Oct. daily 9am-5pm, Nov.-Feb. daily 9am-4pm, adults $14, seniors $10, ages 6-17 $5) offer miles of walking through careful plantings and wild landscapes. The garden map is also a seasonal guide, useful for those who aren't sure whether it's rhododendron season or whether the dahlia garden might be in bloom. Butterflies flutter and bees buzz, and good labels teach novice botany enthusiasts the names of the plants they see. Children can pick up their own brochure, called "Quail Trail: A Child's Guide" and enjoy an exploratory adventure designed just for them.

Entertainment and Events

The **Gloriana Musical Theatre** (210 N. Corry St., 707/964-7469, www.gloriana.org) seeks to bring music and theater to young people, so they produce major musicals that appeal to kids, such as *The Aristocats* and *Charlotte's Web*. On the other hand, *Into the Woods* and the *Rock 'N Roll Revue* appeal mostly to people past their second decade. Local performers star in the two major shows and numerous one-off performances that Gloriana puts on each year.

Art is a big deal in the Mendocino Coast. Accordingly, the area hosts a number of art events each year. **Art in the Gardens** (18220 N. Hwy. 1, Fort Bragg, www.gardenbythesea.org, $20 at the door, $15 in advance) takes place each August at the Mendocino Coast Botanical Gardens, for which it is an annual fundraiser. The gardens are decked out with the finest local artwork, food, and wine, and there is music to entertain the crowds who come to eat, drink, view, and purchase art.

Shopping

If you really enjoyed Glass Beach, you may want to stop in at the **Glass Beach Museum and Gift Shop** (17801 N. Hwy. 1, 707/962-0590, www.glassbeachjewelry.com, daily 10am-5pm), 1.1 miles south of Fort Bragg. You can see a wide array of found treasures from over the years, hear stories from Captain Cass, a retired sailor and expert glass scavenger, and also buy sea glass set in pendants and rings.

Vintage clothing enthusiasts will love **If the Shoe Fits** (337 N. Franklin St., 707/964-2580, daily 10am-5pm). Its eclectic collection of used clothing and accessories for men and women usually includes interesting pieces, well preserved and in good condition.

The place to go on the North Coast to feed your vacation reading habit is—where else?—**The Bookstore** (353 Franklin St., 707/964-6559, daily 10am-5:30pm), a small shop with a well-curated selection of new and used books likely to please discriminating readers. Upstairs is a selection of used records for sale for music lovers.

Sports and Recreation

SPORTFISHING

The Mendocino Coast is an ideal location to watch whales do acrobatics, or to try to land the big one (salmon, halibut, rock cod, or tuna). During Dungeness crab season, you can even go out on a crab boat, learn to set pots, and catch your own delectable delicacy.

Many charters leave out of Noyo Harbor in Fort Bragg. The **Trek II** (Noyo Harbor, 707/964-4550, www.anchorcharterboats.com, daily 7am-8pm, 5-hour fishing trip $80, 2-hour whale-watching $35) offers fishing trips and whale-watching jaunts (Dec.-May). They'll take you rockfishing in summer, crabbing in winter, and chasing after salmon and tuna in season.

The **Noyo Fishing Center** (32440 N. Harbor Dr., Noyo Harbor, 707/964-3000, www.fortbraggfishing.com, half-day fishing trip $65-100, 2-hour whale-watching excursion $35) can take you out salmon fishing or up off the Lost Coast for halibut fishing. They'll help you fish for cod and various deep-sea dwellers in season (May 15-Aug. 15). The crew can even clean and vacuum-pack your catch on the dock before you leave.

HIKING

The hike to take in MacKerricher State Park (Hwy. 1, 707/964-9112, www.parks.ca.gov, visitors center daily 9am-3pm, day use free), three miles north of Fort Bragg, is the **Ten Mile Beach Trail** (10 miles round-trip, moderate), starting at the Laguna Point Parking Area at the north end of Fort Bragg and running five miles up to the Ten Mile River. Most of this path is fairly level and paved. It's an easy walk you can take at your own pace and turn around whenever you want. Street bikes and inline skates are also allowed on this trail.

HORSEBACK RIDING

What better way to enjoy the rugged cliffs, windy beaches, and quiet forests of the coast than on the back of a horse? **Ricochet Ridge Ranch** (24201 N. U.S. 101, 707/964-9669, www.horse-vacation.com) has 10-mile beach trail rides ($50) departing four times a day at 10am, noon, 2pm and 4pm. They also offer longer beach and trail rides, sunset beach rides, and full-fledged riding vacations by reservation (private guided rides $90-310).

SURFING

There are options for surfing in the Fort Bragg area. Just south of town is **Hare Creek** (southwest of the intersection of Hwy. 1 and Hwy. 20, north end of the Hare Creek Bridge), one of the region's most popular spots. North of town is **Virgin Creek** (1.5 miles north of Fort Bragg on Hwy. 1), another well-known break.

The **Lost Surf Shack** (319 N. Franklin St., 707/961-0889, daily 10am-6pm, surfboards $20/day, wetsuits $12.50/day) in downtown Fort Bragg rents surfboards and wetsuits to the surfing inclined.

SPAS

The **Bamboo Garden Spa** (303 N. Main St., Suite C, 707/962-9396, www.bamboogardenspa.com, Tues.-Sat. 10am-8pm, Sun.-Mon. 11am-6:30pm, $80-180) pampers its guests with a wide array of massage, skin, and beauty treatments. Get a 50-minute massage, or try the Balinese Soul Soother or the Vanilla Bean Sugar Scrub.

Accommodations

Stringent zoning laws about development and expansion of businesses in the coastal zone are the main reason you're not likely to find a lot of lodging bargains here; only a few chain hotels have managed to build in Fort Bragg.

UNDER $150

One budget option is the **Surf Motel** (1220 S. Main St., 707/964-5361 or 800/339-5361, www.surfmotelfb.com, $99-275). There's no pool, but the hotel pleases a variety of vacationers by providing a bike-washing station, a fish-cleaning station, an outdoor shower for divers, a garden to stroll through, and an area set aside for horseshoes and barbecues. Your spacious modern guest room comes with breakfast, free wireless Internet access, a microwave,

a fridge, and a blow dryer. If you rent one of the two apartments, you get a whole kitchen and room for four people.

The **Beachcomber Motel** (1111 N. Main St., 707/964-2402, www.thebeachcombermotel.com, $109-259) is clean and decent, offering many rooms with ocean views; pets are allowed in some rooms. Amenities are minimal but acceptable, similar to a low-end chain motel. Expect shampoo and soap in your tiny bath, but little else. Guest rooms are big enough to satisfy, although some visitors find them a bit dark and sparsely furnished. Thin walls and shared patios make noise a problem, and the location at the north end of town makes it a little inconvenient if your goal is to be near downtown Fort Bragg. What really makes the Beachcomber worthwhile, besides its lower-than-B&B prices, is that it's right on Pudding Creek Beach and the popular Ten Mile Beach Trail.

The stately **Grey Whale Inn** (615 N. Main St., 800/382-7244, www.greywhaleinn.com, $135-171) was once a community hospital. The blocky craftsman-style building was erected by the Union Lumber Company in 1915. Today, 13 spacious, simply appointed guest rooms welcome travelers. Whether you get a view of the water or a more pedestrian city view, you'll have a lovely, individually decorated guest room with a private bath and queen or king bed, perhaps covered by an old-fashioned quilt. The inn prides itself on simplicity and friendliness, and its perfect location in downtown Fort Bragg makes visitors feel at home walking to dinner or the beach. It also has a unique feature for an inn: a game room with a pool table and foosball.

$150-250

◀ **Weller House** (524 Stewart St., 707/964-4415, www.wellerhouse.com, $180-280) is a picture-perfect B&B with elegantly restored Victorian-style guest rooms, ocean views, and sumptuous home cooking. There are even a few gloriously secluded guest rooms for rent up in the old water tower, which is the high point in the whole city of Fort Bragg. If you can't finish writing your novel here, you're just not trying. But that's not all: The manager, Vivien LaMothe, is also a tango dancer, and the third floor of the main building—a gorgeous 1886 mansion listed on the National Register of Historic Places—is, believe it or not, a ballroom (although the original owner, Mr. Weller, manager of the old company store for the mill, was a strict Baptist and used it for Sunday school). The virgin redwood floor, the outstanding acoustics, and the spacious porch where dancers can step out for a breath of air make it a marvelous place for a milonga. Some of the great tango dancers think so too—they come from the Bay Area and far beyond to participate in monthly tango weekends and twice a year tango festivals. Check the website for schedules, celebrity dance teachers, and chamber music concerts. Weller House is one block west of Main Street, in view of the Skunk Train depot, and an easy walk to good restaurants and shopping.

Camping

MacKerricher State Park (Hwy. 1, 707/964-9112, www.parks.ca.gov, reservations 800/444-7275, www.reserveamerica.com, $35), three miles north of Fort Bragg, is also a fine place to spend a night or two as you explore the area. Reservations are recommended April 1-October 15, and they're site-specific. In the winter season, camping is available on a first-come, first-served basis. The park has 107 sites suitable for tents and RVs up to 35 feet in its wooded and pleasant West Pinewood Campground; there are also a group campground and walk-in hike-and-bike sites. Restrooms with flush toilets as well as hot showers are provided, and each campsite has a fire ring, picnic table, and food storage locker.

Food

It used to be that you had to go to the village of Mendocino for a restaurant meal, but lately Fort Bragg has developed a more-than-respectable culinary scene of its own. Many excellent restaurants are available within a few blocks of the town center and beach.

AMERICAN

Upstairs in an old Fort Bragg lumber building, the **◖Mendo Bistro** (301 N. Main St. #J, 707/964-4974, http://mendobistro.com, daily 5pm-9pm, $15-32) has the sort of menu one might expect in a bigger city. One of the best parts of the menu is the "Choice" section, where you choose the style of meat, seafood, or vegetarian option and how it is cooked along with what sauce it is cooked in. The hormone- and antibiotic-free steaks are perfectly cooked and delicious. There are also a great deal of vegetarian offerings on the menu—from an eggplant trio entrée to several meat-free pastas—but the one veggie item to seek out is the Bistro's polenta whether it's the polenta croutons in the Caesar salad or the creamy polenta that comes as a side dish. Before opening Mendo Bistro in 1999, chef Nicholas Petti was a touring musician and onetime member of the seminal alt country band Whiskeytown.

The **North Coast Brewing Company** (444 N. Main St., 707/964-3400, www.northcoastbrewing.com, Wed.-Thurs. and Sun. 4pm-9:30pm, Fri.-Sat. 4pm-10pm, $15-33) opened in 1988, aiming at the then-nascent artisanal beer market. Today, they also serve seafood, steak, and creative salads. Of course, it's best to wash down your beer with a North Coast microbrew. You can taste the magic in their Red Seal Ale, Old Rasputin Russian Imperial Stout, and Scrimshaw Pilsner.

The most popular burger in town is at **Jenny's Giant Burger** (940 N. Main St., 707/964-2235, daily 10:30am-9pm, $2.50-7). This little place has a 1950s hamburger-stand feel, but there's nothing stale about it. The burgers are fresh and antibiotic-free, with garden burger and veggie sandwich options. Jenny's followers are devoted, so it can get crowded, but there are a few outdoor tables, and you can always get your treats to go.

BAKERIES AND CAFES

Despite the often drizzly overcast weather, Mendocino Coast residents and visitors crave ice cream in the summer just like anyone else. **Cowlick's Ice Cream** (250 N. Main St.,

707/962-9271, www.cowlicksicecream.com, daily 11am-9pm) serves delectable handmade ice cream in a variety of flavors. Yes, they really do serve mushroom ice cream during the famous fall Mendo mushroom season. You can get the perennial favorite flavors such as vanilla, chocolate, coffee, and strawberry. If you're lucky, you might also find your favorite seasonal flavor (banana daiquiri, cinnamon, green tea) when you visit. If you're not in downtown Fort Bragg, you can also find this local family-owned chain at the Mendocino Coast Botanical Gardens (18220 N. Hwy. 1); at **Frankie's Ice Cream Parlor** (44951 Ukiah St., Mendocino, 707/937-2436, www.frankiesmendocino.com, daily 11am-9pm) in Mendocino Village; on the Skunk Train; and at **J. D. Redhouse** (212 S. Main St., Willits, 707/459-1214, daily 10am-6pm).

If you're more interested in coffee and pastries than a temporary office space, the **Headlands Coffeehouse** (120 E. Laurel St., 707/964-1987, www.headlandscoffeehouse.com, Mon.-Sat. 7am-10pm, Sun. 7am-7pm) is unquestionably the place to go in Fort Bragg. They have around 15 different self-serve roasts of coffee and food ranging from breakfast burritos to paninis. There is free live music in the evenings and free Internet access. So what's the catch? There are no electrical outlets available for customers, so you can only use your laptop as long as your battery lasts.

If what you're really looking for is a place to spread out and work while having coffee and snacks as a bonus, head to the **Mendocino Cookie Company/Zappa's Coffee** (301 N. Main St., 707/964-0282, www.menodcinocookies.com, daily 7am-6pm). For a minimal fee they'll let you rent one of their computers, or stay as long as you like in the large atrium area they share with several other businesses, which has free Internet access, plenty of electrical outlets, and elbow room. Oh, and the fresh-baked cookies taste as good as they smell.

BREAKFAST
Egghead's (326 N. Main St., 707/964-5005, www.eggheadsrestaurant.com, daily 7am-2pm, $6-19) has been serving an enormous menu of breakfast, lunch, and brunch items to satisfy diners for more than 30 years. The menu includes every imaginable omelet combination, cinnamon raisin toast, burritos, Reuben sandwiches, and "flying-monkey potatoes," derived from the *Wizard of Oz* theme that runs through the place.

FARMERS MARKET
Fort Bragg hosts a **farmers market** (Franklin St. between Laurel and Pine, www.mcfarm.org, May-Oct. Wed. 3pm-6pm) that sells lots of good stuff, including wild caught seafood, free range beef, and fresh baked bread.

ITALIAN
Small and almost always packed, the **Piaci Pub & Pizzeria** (120 W. Redwood Ave., 707/961-1133, www.piacipizza.com, Mon.-Wed. 11am-9:30pm, Thurs.-Sat. 11am-10pm, Sun. 4pm-9:30pm, $9-26) has 16 pizzas in three different sizes along with an array of salads, calzones, and focaccia breads with toppings. The pizzas range from traditional pepperoni to more creative options like pesto, chevre, pears, prosciutto, and herbs. Piaci has an extensive list of brews, from Belgian-style beers to hearty ales.

JAPANESE
Taka's Grill (250A N. Main St., 707/964-5204, daily noon-9pm, $12-20) fills up for lunch. Dine in the small indoor area or in the adjacent atrium. The fresh rolls include a flavor-filled mango salmon roll.

MEXICAN
Inside a Fort Bragg strip mall, **Los Gallitos** (130 S. Main St., 707/964-4519, Mon.-Sat. 11am-8pm, Sun. 10am-8pm, $7-16, cash only) doesn't look like much. But you know this is a better-than-average taqueria when the thick fresh tortilla strips and superb salsa hit your table. Everything on the menu, from burritos to tostados is what you'd expect, but the attention to little details like the grilled onions and beans on the very tasty carne asada torta make this place special.

SEAFOOD

With the small fishing and crabbing fleet of Fort Bragg's Noyo Harbor, it's natural that lots of seafood restaurants are clustered nearby. Head down to the harbor where any one of the several casual restaurants and fish markets offer the most authentic, freshest, and simplest preparations of salmon, mussels, and Dungeness crab in season. One spot known for its fish and chips is the **Sea Pal Cove Restaurant** (32390 N. Harbor Dr., 707/964-1300, Wed.-Thurs. noon-5pm, Fri.-Sun. noon-7pm, $6-13, cash only).

THAI

Small and unassuming, but well worth a visit, **Nit's Café** (322 Main St., 707/964-7187, Wed.-Sun. 5:30pm-9pm, $14-26, cash only) specializes in Thai and Asian fusion. Noted for its beautiful presentations of both classic and creative dishes, Nit's gets rave reviews from nearly everyone who tries it.

Information and Services

The **Mendocino Coast Chamber of Commerce and Visitors Center** (217 S. Main St., 707/961-6300, www.mendocinocoast.com, Mon.-Fri. 9am-5pm, Sat. 10am-3pm) has unusually attentive and well-trained staff in addition to all the maps, brochures, and ideas you could possibly want. This operation also serves as the Mendocino County film office, which strongly encourages filmmaking in the area. Come in and get the inside story on where to see the filming locations of *Summer of '42,* in which the bluffs of Fort Bragg play the role of Long Island; *East of Eden; Karate Kid III; Humanoids from the Deep;* and many more. Films have been made around here since the beginning of the silent era, as have television shows. The staff can even direct you to Angela Lansbury's typewriter from *Murder, She Wrote* or to the Skunk Train, which appeared in *The Majestic* with Jim Carrey.

Of all the towns on the Mendocino Coast, Fort Bragg has the most urban atmosphere, complete with supermarkets, big-box stores, and a **post office** (203 N. Franklin St.,

707/964-2302, www.usps.com, Mon.-Fri. 8:30am-5pm).

The **Mendocino Coast District Hospital** (700 River Dr. at Cypress St., 707/961-1234, www.mcdh.org) has the nearest full-service emergency room.

Getting There and Around

Fort Bragg is located on Highway 1; driving here from San Francisco takes about 4 hours. There is no "fast" way to reach Fort Bragg. The road from any direction is narrow and full of curves, at least for an hour or two, so be prepared to make the scenic journey part of the fun. From Willits, take Highway 20 (Fort Bragg-Willits Rd.) west for 30 miles. If ever a road could be described as sun-dappled, this is one. The sun pops in and out among the redwood forest and makes you want to use all the pullouts to take photos. Keep in mind that there is no cell-phone service along this road, so it is not a good place to run out of gas. Allow plenty of time—it takes longer than you'd expect to travel these 30 miles.

As one of the largest towns in the region, Fort Bragg has access to more public transportation. The most enjoyable way to get here is to take the **Skunk Train** (866/457-5865, www.skunktrain.com) from Willits. The **Mendocino Transit Authority** (707/462-1422 or 800/696-4682, www.mta4.org) has a number of bus lines that pass through Fort Bragg, and it also offers **Dial-a-Ride Curb-to-Curb Service** (707/964-1800). The most common way to get to and around Fort Bragg, however, is by car.

Westport

The next town north along Highway 1 is Westport, 16 miles north of Fort Bragg, with its own patch of ocean, a few essential services, and one gem. It's the last settlement before the wild Lost Coast. The motto at the **Ⓒ Westport Hotel** (3892 Hwy. 1, 707/964-3688 or 877/964-3688, www.westporthotel.us, $140-195) is, "At last, you've found nowhere." The Westport Hotel is marvelous and private, perfect for a honeymoon spent in luxury and comfort. Each of the six guest rooms has one bed and a bath with fixtures that blend perfectly into the historic 1890 house. Some guest rooms have small private balconies overlooking the waves, and all guests have access to the redwood sauna. Fresh scones, fruit, and coffee are delivered to your room in the morning, and a full hot breakfast is served in the dining room.

Inside the Westport Hotel is the **Old Abalone Pub** (3892 Hwy. 1, 707/964-3688 or 877/964-3688, www.westporthotel.us, Thurs.-Mon. 5pm-9pm, afternoon tea Sat. 3pm-5pm, brunch Sun. 10am-2pm, dinner $10-25). Thanks to a large mirror over the bar, everyone in the dining room gets an ocean view—even those seated with their backs to the sea.

Camping is available two miles north of Westport at **Westport-Union Landing State Beach** (Hwy. 1, 707/937-5804, www.parks. ca.gov, $25), with 86 first-come, first-served sites. There are no showers or other amenities, just the cliffs, the waves, the sunsets, and the views.

Mendocino Wine Country

Mendocino's interior valley might not be quite as glamorous as the coast, but it is home to history, art, and liquor. The Anderson Valley is the apex of Mendocino's wine region, although the tiny town of Hopland also has its share of tasting rooms. Ukiah, the county seat, is home to a number of microbreweries and a thriving agricultural industry. Up in determinedly funky Willits, a late-1960s art vibe thrives in the 21st century.

Unlike the chilly windy coast, the interior valleys of Mendocino get hot in the summer. Bring shorts, a swimsuit, and an air-conditioned car if you plan to visit June-September.

ANDERSON VALLEY

The Anderson Valley wine trail, also known as Highway 128, begins in Boonville and continues northwest toward the coast, with most of the wineries clustered between Boonville and Navarro.

Wineries

A big name in the Anderson Valley, **Scharffenberger Cellars** (8501 Hwy. 128, Philo, 707/895-2957, www.scharffenbergercellars.com, daily 11am-5pm, tasting $3) makes wine in Mendocino. The tasting room is elegant and unusually child-friendly.

A broad-ranging winery with a large estate vineyard and event center, **Navarro Vineyards** (5601 Hwy. 128, Philo, 707/895-3686 or 800/537-9463, www.navarrowine.com, summer daily 9am-6pm, winter daily 9am-5pm, tasting free) offers a range of tasty wines as well as some interesting specialty products such as the non-alcoholic verjus.

In a valley full of great wineries, **Roederer Estate** (4501 Hwy. 128, 707/895-2288, www. roedererestate.com, daily 11am-5pm, tasting $6) sparkles. The California sparkling wines it creates are some of the best you'll taste. The large tasting room features a bar with sweeping views of the estate vineyards and huge cases filled with Roederer's well-deserved awards. Pourers are knowledgeable, and you'll get to taste from magnum bottles—a rarity at any winery. Be sure to ask for a taste of Roederer's rarely seen still wines; you might find something wonderful.

Small boutique wineries are clustered in the Anderson Valley, an area less crowded than Napa or Sonoma. Any of these are worth a visit to seek out gem wines that aren't available in shops. **Esterlina** (1200 Holmes Ranch Rd., Philo, 707/895-2920, www.esterlinavineyards. com, tasting by appointment only, reserve tasting $15 pp, waived with purchase) offers the best view in the valley—come around sunset if you can. Beyond the spectacular vineyard vistas, Esterlina provides tastes of a selection of sparkling and still wines that make it well worth the trip to the top of its hill.

Handley Cellars (3151 Hwy. 128, Philo, 707/895-3876 or 800/733-3151, www.

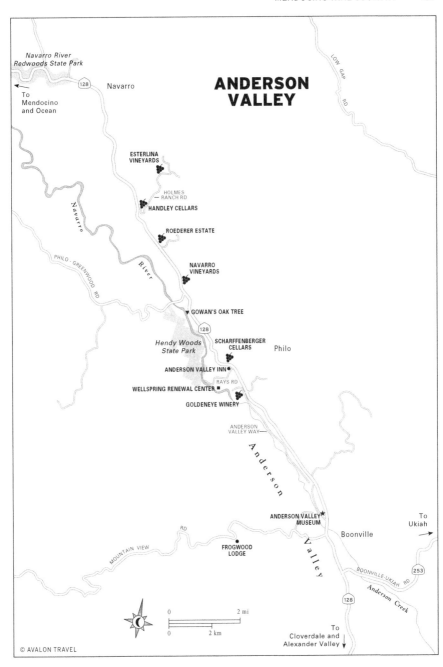

Navarro River
Redwoods State Park

128   Navarro

To
Mendocino
and Ocean

ANDERSON VALLEY

LOW GAP RD

Navarro

ESTERLINA
VINEYARDS

HOLMES
RANCH RD

HANDLEY CELLARS

River

PHILO - GREENWOOD RD

ROEDERER ESTATE

NAVARRO
VINEYARDS

GOWAN'S OAK TREE

128

Hendy Woods
State Park

SCHARFFENBERGER
CELLARS

Philo

ANDERSON VALLEY INN

RAYS RD

WELLSPRING RENEWAL CENTER

GOLDENEYE WINERY

ANDERSON
VALLEY WAY

Anderson

MOUNTAIN VIEW   RD

FROGWOOD
LODGE

ANDERSON VALLEY
MUSEUM

Valley

Boonville

To
Ukiah

BOONVILLE - UKIAH RD

253

Anderson Creek

128

To
Cloverdale and
Alexander Valley

0   2 mi

0   2 km

© AVALON TRAVEL

Enjoy beer and disc golf at the Anderson Valley Brewing Company.

handleycellars.com, May-Oct. daily 10am-6pm, Nov.-Apr. daily 10am-5pm) offers a complimentary tasting of handcrafted wines you probably won't see in grocery stores. The intriguing Handley tasting room features folk art from around the world for sale. Books on wine are sold too, especially those that focus on women making and drinking wine.

For visitors who prefer a cold beer to a glass of wine, **⟨ Anderson Valley Brewing Company** (17700 Hwy. 253, Boonville, 707/895-2337, www.avbc.com, Apr.-Dec. daily 11am-6pm, Jan.-Mar. Thurs.-Mon. 11am-6pm) serves up an array of microbrews that changes each year and each season. The warehouse-size beer hall feels like a wine tasting room and has a bar, a number of tables, and a good-size gift shop. A beer garden out back is comfortable in spring and fall, and the disc golf course is popular with travelers and locals alike.

Sports and Recreation

The best hiking and biking trails in the area are in and around the Anderson Valley, where evergreen forests shade hikers from the worst of the summer heat. At **Hendy Redwoods State Park** (Philo-Greenwood Rd., 0.5 miles south of Hwy. 128, 707/895-3141 in summer, Mendocino district office 707/937-5804, www.parks.ca.gov, daily 8am-sunset, $8), you can hike to two old-growth redwood groves. For an easy, shaded walk, visit the **Big Hendy** grove and enjoy its self-guided nature trail, which is wheelchair accessible and perfect for a sedate forest walk. Another good short hike with just a little slope is the moderate **Hermit's Hut Trail**—yes, Hendy used to have its very own hermit. No one resides in the tree-stump hut anymore, although it remains a curiosity for hikers. Fit hikers who want a longer trek can weave around the whole park; **Big Hendy Loop** connects to the Fire Road, which connects to the Hermit's Hut Trail, which intersects the Azalea Loop and runs down to the **Little Hendy Loop** for a complete survey of the park's best regions. With the Navarro River running along the length of the park, swimming, kayaking, and canoeing are possible in Hendy Redwoods at certain times of the year.

© SHANE DOLBIER

NORTH COAST BREWERIES

While Napa Valley is known for its wine, California's North Coast is known for its beer. Here local craft beer and microbrews are served in restaurants and line the beer aisles of local supermarkets. One way to get a taste of these beers or to sample their smaller batches is to visit a North Coast brewery or brewpub.

If you're a beer fan, the **Anderson Valley Brewing Company's Tap Room and Brewery** (17700 Hwy. 253, Boonville, 707/895-2337, www.avbc.com, Apr.-Dec. daily 11am-6pm, Jan.-Mar. Thurs.-Mon. 11am-6pm) is well worth a visit. With its high ceilings and copper bar, the taproom feels like an informal tasting room in a winery. They have 20 taps that serve Anderson Valley favorites like Boont Amber Ale, along with 10 taps that feature rotating smaller batch brews including a sour stout. There's more to do at Anderson Valley than just drinking their tasty beers. Brewery tours ($5) are offered every day the taproom is open at 1:30pm and 3pm, while you can also grab a beer and head outdoors to play the brewery's 18-hole disc golf course ($5).

Since opening in 1988, the **North Coast Brewing Company** (455 N. Main St., Fort Bragg, 707/964-2739, www.northcoastbrewing.com, Taproom & Grill Wed.-Thurs. and Sun. 4pm-9:30pm, Fri.-Sat. 4pm-10pm) has expanded so that it takes up all four corners of a Fort Bragg city block with the actual brewery, the brewery shop, and the taproom and grill. Head into the popular taproom to try North Coast favorites including the Red Seal Ale or the more potent Brother Thelonious Belgian Style Abbey Ale.

If you crave sustainable suds, visit the **Eel River Brewing Company's Taproom & Grill** (1777 Alamar Way, Fortuna, 707/725-2739, http://eelriverbrewing.com, daily 11am-11pm), where you can sip organic beer that was made with renewable energy. Drink the Organic IPA or Organic Acai Berry Wheat Ale at the taproom's long wooden bar or head outside to drink in the adjacent beer garden. To tour the brewing facilities in the nearby town of Scotia, contact the company (707/764-1772) during weekday business hours.

The **Lost Coast Brewery & Café** (617 4th St., Eureka, 707/445-4480, www.lostcoast.com, Sun.-Thurs. 11am-10pm, Fri.-Sat. 11am-11pm) feels like a local's bar. The hockey stick-shaped bar and restaurant is filled with people even on weeknights. The brewery's Great White and Lost Coast Pale Ale are the most popular brews, but the smooth Downtown Brown is recommended for darker beer fans.

A few miles inland, the **Mad River Brewing Company Tasting Room** (101 Taylor Way, Blue Lake, 707/668-4151 Ext. 106, www.madriverbrewing.com, Mon.-Fri. 1pm-9pm, Sat. noon-9pm, Sun. noon-8pm) has almost nightly live music to entertain you while you enjoy their Steelhead Extra Pale Ale or Jamaica Red Ale. **Tours** (707/668-4151 Ext. 105, daily 1pm-4pm, free) are also offered daily.

A new craft beer operation that Humboldt County brew fans rave about is the Redwood Curtain Brewing Company. **The Redwood Curtain Brewing Company Tasting Room** (550 S. G St., Arcata, 707/826-7222, www.redwoodcurtainbrewing.com, call or visit website for hours) is the place to try their Imperial Golden Ale or the creative Cerise Coup, which is aged in a French oak chardonnay barrel and then left with cherries for six months. They don't even bottle their beer yet.

Accommodations

Lodging options in and around the Anderson Valley vary widely. In the valley proper you're likely to find funky hotels, cabins, and forest-shaded campgrounds.

The **Anderson Valley Inn** (8480 Hwy. 128, Philo, 707/895-3325, www.avinn.com, $85-180), between Boonville and Philo, makes the perfect spot from which to divide your time between the Anderson Valley and the Mendocino Coast. Six small guest rooms are done up in bright colors, homey bedspreads, and attractive appointments in this small multiple-building inn. A butterfly-filled garden invites guests to sit out on the porches reading the paper and sipping coffee. The two two-bedroom suites have full kitchens and are perfect for travelers looking to stay in the area a bit longer. The friendly owners welcome children and dogs in the suites—both must be attended at all times—and can be very helpful with hints about how best to explore the region. This inn often fills quickly on summer weekends, as it's one of the best-value accommodations in the region. There's a two-night minimum on weekends April-November.

In the middle of Boonville, the quaint **Boonville Hotel** (14050 Hwy. 128, 707/895-2210, www.boonvillehotel.com, $125-350) has a rough weathered exterior that contrasts interestingly with the 15 updated contemporary guest rooms, each of which is bright and airy with earth-tone furniture and an attractive collection of mismatched decorations. If you're traveling with children or pets, request one of the guest rooms set up to accommodate them. Downstairs, you'll find comfortable spacious common areas and a huge garden suitable for strolling. Amenities include a bookshop and a gift shop, a good-size bar, and a dining room. For a relaxing treat, book one of the guest rooms with a balcony, which comes with a hammock set up and ready for napping, or a guest room with an outdoor bathtub for soaking and relaxing.

Camping

Stylish lodgings aren't common in the Anderson Valley, but you can still find a pleasant place to stay near the wineries. For wine and nature lovers on a budget, the campgrounds at **Indian Creek County Park** (Hwy. 128 at mile marker 23.48, 1 mile east of Philo, 707/463-4291, www.co.mendocino.ca.us, $20) and **Hendy Woods State Park** (Philo-Greenwood Rd., 0.5 miles south of Hwy. 128, 8 miles northwest of Boonville, 707/895-3141, www.parks.ca.gov, $20) provide woodsy, shady campsites.

Food

A picnic makes a perfect lunch in the Anderson Valley, and farmers markets and farm stands can supply fresh local ingredients. The **Boonville Farmers Market** (14050 Hwy. 128, Boonville, www.mcfarm.org, May-Oct. Sat. 9:30am-noon) draws a crowd, so be prepared to hunt for parking. For fresh fruit and vegetables every day, try **Gowan's Oak Tree Farm Stand** (6600 Hwy. 128, 2.5 miles north of Philo, 707/895-3353, daily 8am-7pm). The stand belongs to the local Gowan's Oak Tree Farm and sells only in-season local produce and homemade products made with the same fruits and veggies.

For an elegant full-service dining experience, enjoy **Table 128** (14050 Hwy. 128, Boonville, 707/895-2210, www.boonvillehotel.com, by reservation only Apr.-Nov. Thurs.-Mon., Dec.-Mar. Fri.-Sun., $40-50), the restaurant at the Boonville Hotel. Table 128 is family-style and the menu is prix fixe. The food is so fresh and seasonal that the chef won't commit to a menu more than a week in advance, but you can sign up on the website to receive regular menus by email. Reservations are required and must be secured with a credit card for parties of five or more.

Getting There and Around

You can see pretty much all of Anderson Valley from the "wine road," Highway 128. You can get to Highway 128 from U.S. 101 either directly out of Hopland or from Ukiah on Highway 253. From Hopland, take Mountain House Road west for nine miles. Turn right onto Highway 128 and continue north for about 20 miles.

From Ukiah, take U.S. 101 south for three miles. Merge onto Highway 253 and head west for about 17 miles. When you reach Highway 128, turn right. The center of Boonville is less than one mile away.

Many of the major wine-country touring outfits that operate from San Francisco and the Napa Valley also offer trips in the Anderson Valley. **Mendo Wine Tours** (707/937-6700 or 888/805-8687, www.mendowinetours.com, group tours $175 pp, private limo tours $550 for 2 people) is a regional specialist that offers a Lincoln Town Car for small groups and an SUV limo for groups of up to 10.

HOPLAND

Hopland is inland on U.S. 101 about 15 miles south of Ukiah and 28 miles east of the Anderson Valley via Highway 253. Highway 175 leads east to Clear Lake, under 20 miles away.

Solar Living Center

The **Solar Living Center** (13771 S. U.S. 101, 707/472-2450, http://solarliving.org, daily 9am-6pm) is a "12-acre sustainable living demonstration site," showing, among other things, what life might be like without petroleum. The center has exhibits on permaculture, an organic garden, and a demonstration of solar-powered water systems. The **Real Goods** store (707/472-2403) on the property is also a draw for visitors, and the completely recycled restrooms are worth a look even if you don't need one. If your vehicle happens to run on biodiesel, you can fill your tank here.

For more than 15 years, the Solar Living Center has taken a weekend in August to put on "the greenest show on earth," **MoonDance Eco-Fest** (www.solarliving.org). The hundreds of displays, demonstrations, and workshops go far beyond solar power to teach and exemplify the ever-expanding world of permaculture and renewable energy. Keynote speakers each year include top names from the world of ecological activism and science. But it's not all serious business at Eco-Fest; musicians perform on the main stage, and the Saturday Night Moondance features entertainment and DJs for eco-lovers who want to dance deep into the night.

Wineries

To get to the best wineries in Hopland, you don't even need to leave U.S. 101. The highway runs through the center of town, and almost all the tasting rooms are located along it. For those who love wine but not crowds, the tiny wineries and tasting rooms in Hopland are the perfect place to relax, enjoy sipping each vintage, and really chat with the pourer, who just might be the winemaker and owner. **Graziano** (13251 S. U.S. 101, 707/744-8466,

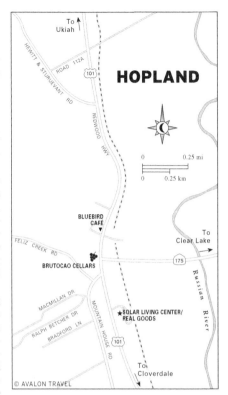

www.grazianofamilyofwines.com, daily 10am-5pm), for example, provides a great small-winery experience.

The star of this mini region is **Brutocao Cellars** (13500 S. U.S. 101, 800/433-3689, www.brutocaocellars.com, daily 10am-5pm, tasting free), whose vineyards crowd the land surrounding the town. It took over the old high school to create its tasting room and restaurant complex. The wide stone-tiled tasting room houses exceptional wines poured by knowledgeable staff. A sizeable gift shop offers gourmet goodies under the Brutocao label, and there are six regulation bocce ball courts if you want to do some lawn bowling with your wine sipping. And if you can't get enough of Brutocao, there is a second tasting room in the Anderson Valley (7000 Hwy. 128, Philo, 800/661-2103, www.

BOONTLING: THE NORTH COAST DIALECT

Take your oddly broken English, throw in some old Scottish and Irish, add a pinch of Spanish and a dash of Pomo, then season with real names and allusions to taste. Speak among friends and family in an isolated community for a dozen years or more. The results: Boontling.

Boontling is a unique and almost dead language developed by the denizens of the then-remote town of Boonville in the Anderson Valley late in the 19th century. The beginnings of Boontling are obscured by time since all the originators of the language are "piked for dusties" – that is, in the cemetery. And many Boonters – speakers of Boontling – are intensely protective of the local lingo. But in the 1960s, Professor Charles C. Adams of Cal State Chico came to town to study the language. He gradually gained the trust of the locals, and was able to write a doctoral thesis, eventually published as a book, *Boontling: An American Lingo*. The book documents the history and acts as a dictionary for the more than 1,000 Boontling terms on record.

So if you find yourself in Anderson Valley drinking "zeese" (coffee) or "aplenty bahl steinber horn" (a really great beer) and hear older folks speaking a language like none you've ever heard, you might just be listening to a rare and endangered conversation in Boontling.

brutocaocellars.com, daily 10am-5pm, tasting free).

Heading north out of town, the highway passes through acres of vineyards spreading out toward the forest in all directions. Many of these grapes belong to **Jeriko** (12141 Hewlett and Sturtevant Rd., 707/744-1140, www.jerikoestate.com, summer daily 10am-5pm, winter noon-5pm, tasting $10). Visitors drive between the chardonnay and the pinot to get to the immense Napa-style tasting room. A glass wall exposes the barrel room with aging wines stacked high, tempting tasters to learn their secrets.

Food

With the closing of the Hopland Inn, Hopland lost some of its best dining and one of its only places to stay. A casual place that most people enjoy is the **Bluebird Café & Catering Company** (13340 S. U.S. 101, 707/744-1633, Mon.-Thurs. 7am-2pm, Fri.-Sun. 7am-7pm, $17-20). Your best bet for a good night's sleep is to stay in Ukiah or Lakeport.

UKIAH

The largest city in Mendocino County, Ukiah is also the county seat. It's known for its wine production.

Sights

SAGELY CITY OF 10,000 BUDDHAS

There's plenty to interest the spiritually curious at the **Sagely City of 10,000 Buddhas** (4951 Bodhi Way, 707/462-0939, www.cttbusa.org, daily 8am-6pm). This active Buddhist college and monastery asks that guests wear modest clothing (avoid short shorts and short skirts, bare chests, and skimpy tank tops) and keep their voices down out of respect for the nuns and monks who make their lives here. The showpiece is the temple, which really does contain 10,000 golden Buddha statues. An extensive gift- and bookshop provides slightly silly souvenirs as well as serious scholarly texts on Buddhism. For a treat, stop in for lunch at the **Jyun Kang Vegetarian Restaurant** (707/468-7966, Wed.-Mon. noon-3pm, $7) on the grounds, which is open to the public.

GRACE HUDSON MUSEUM AND SUN HOUSE

One of the few truly cultural offerings in Ukiah is the **Grace Hudson Museum** (431 S. Main St., 707/467-2836, www.gracehudsonmuseum.org, Wed.-Sat. 10am-4:30pm, Sun. noon-4:30pm, adults $4, seniors and students $3, family $10). This small set of galleries focuses on the life and work of the artist Grace

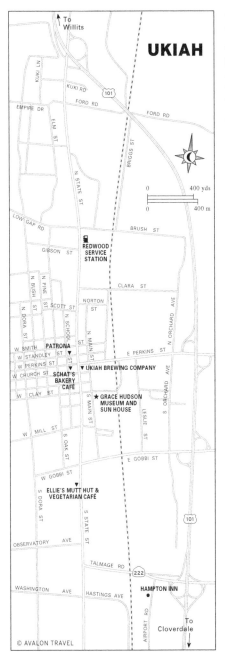

Hudson and her husband, Dr. John Hudson. The life's work of this couple included the study of the Pomo people and other Native American groups. The museum's permanent collection includes many of Grace's paintings, a number of Pomo baskets, and the works of dozens of other California artists. The 1911 craftsman-style **Sun House,** adjacent to the main museum building, was the Hudsons' home, and docent-guided tours are available.

Entertainment and Events

Ukiah Brewing Company (102 S. State St., 707/468-5898, www.ukiahbrewingco.com, kitchen Sun.-Thurs. 11am-9pm, Fri.-Sat. 11am-10pm, bar Mon.-Thurs. 11am-11pm, Fri.-Sun. 11am-1am, $8-11) offers good beer and good entertainment several nights each week. Settle in with a pilsner or amber ale and enjoy the live music and other weekend-evening entertainment. You might even get a chance to sing at the Wednesday open mics.

Sports and Recreation

Lake Mendocino is an artificial lake along the Russian River that is held in place by Coyote Dam. It's just off U.S. 101 north of Ukiah, allowing residents and visitors the chance to powerboat, water-ski, canoe, kayak, fish, and play a round of disc golf. Shockingly uncrowded even on the hottest summer afternoons, this is a great spot to cool off. You can even find a few beaches and lawns on which to spread out a blanket and lie down, and shaded picnic tables where you can enjoy lunch.

You can access the lake from Lake Mendocino Drive, Calpella Drive, and a few other local roads off U.S. 101. Five marinas catering to boaters and two boat ramps are along the shores of the lake. A number of campgrounds also circle the lake—some are boat-in only.

A great place to take a nice cool and shady hike is **Montgomery Woods State Nature Reserve** (Orr Springs Rd., 707/937-5804, www.parks.ca.gov, free), 13 miles west of Ukiah. This remote redwoods park is less crowded than its more accessible and more popular brethren.

The quintessential hike at Montgomery runs along **Montgomery Creek** (3 miles, moderate), where you get a chance to see something special and unusual—both the coastal and giant-sequoia species of redwood tree growing in the same park. Montgomery's location and climate make it hospitable to both types, which usually grow hundreds of miles apart.

There is a tranquil and serene (most of the time) historic spa at the edge of Ukiah. Since its establishment in 1854, **Vichy Springs** (2605 Vichy Springs Rd., 707/462-9515, www.vichysprings.com, daily 9am-dusk, treatments $105-195 per hour, baths $50 per day) has been patronized by Mark Twain, Jack London, Ulysses S. Grant, Teddy Roosevelt, and California governor Jerry Brown. The hot springs, mineral-heavy and naturally carbonated, closely resemble the world-famous waters of their namesake at Vichy in France. Services include the baths, a hot pool, and an Olympic-size swimming pool as well as a day spa.

In downtown Ukiah, **Tranquility Day Spa** (203 S. State St., 707/463-2189, http://tranquilitydayspaukiah.com, Mon.-Fri. 10am-5:30pm, Sat. 11am-3pm) caters to the hippie side of this culturally mixed town. Swirling curtains and sandalwood incense pervade the big warehouse space. Tranquility has both salon and spa services for one-stop shopping for a mud mask, a hot-stone massage, a haircut, a Brazilian wax, a reflexology treatment, and even a "Tango Paraffin Bodyfango," with specific services for men, women, and teens.

Accommodations

There are plenty of lodgings in Ukiah, although they tend to be mostly standard chain motels. Out by the airport, the **Fairfield Inn** (1140 Airport Park Blvd., 707/463-3600, www.marriott.com, $99-150) is a good choice. With an elegant lobby, an indoor pool and spa, a small exercise room, and a generous complimentary continental breakfast, it has what you need to be comfortable. The guest rooms are what you'd expect of a decent mid-range chain: floral bedspreads, durable nondescript carpet, and clean baths. Next door, the **Hampton Inn** (1160 Airport Park Blvd., 707/263-0889, www.hamptoninn.com, $99-149) offers attractive guest rooms, an outdoor heated pool, high-speed Internet access, a buffet breakfast, and a courtyard with koi ponds.

If you're coming to town for a peaceful retreat, the best choice may be **Vichy Springs Resort** (2605 Vichy Springs Rd., 707/462-9515, www.vichysprings.com, $135-390). The guest rooms, in a genteel and rustic old inn and nearby cottages, are small but comfortable, with private baths, warm bedspreads, and cool breezes, and many have views of the mountains or creek. Use of all the pools and hiking trails on the 700-acre grounds along with Internet access and a buffet breakfast are included in the rates.

Food

A local favorite, the **Maple Restaurant** (295 S. State St., 707/462-5221, daily 7am-2pm, $10) serves excellent and inexpensive breakfasts and lunches. Excellent service complements good uncomplicated American-style food. Shockingly good coffee is a final charming touch to this lovely find.

For a cool relaxing breather on a hot Ukiah day, stop in at one of the three locations of **Schat's Bakery Café** (113 W. Perkins St., 707/462-1670, Mon.-Fri. 5:30am-6pm, Sat. 5:30am-5pm, www.schats.com; 1255A Airport Park Blvd., 707/468-5850, Mon.-Fri. 7am-8pm, Sat. 7am-7pm, Sun. 8am-7pm; 1000 Hensley Creek Rd., 707/468-3145, Mon.-Thurs. 7am-8:15pm, Fri. 7am-3pm, $5-12). They'll make you a quick, filling sandwich on fresh-baked bread, and you can hang out as long as you want in the large, airy dining rooms.

Ellie's Mutt Hut & Vegetarian Café (732 S. State St., 707/468-5376, http://elliesmutthutukiahca.com, Mon.-Sat. 6:30am-8pm, $8-15) has great vegetarian entrées and an impressive hot dog list. It's one of the best places in California for a mixed group of conscientious vegans and couldn't-care-less carnivores to have a good time together; Ellie's is one of the things that make Ukiah Ukiah. The atmosphere is hamburger-stand casual, and the food is mostly healthy.

Of the dining options in Ukiah, one of the very best is **Patrona** (130 W. Standley St., 707/462-9181, www.patronarestaurant.com, Mon.-Sat. 11am-5pm and 5:30pm-9pm, Sun. 9am-5pm and 5:30pm-9pm, $13-29), where especially innovative California cuisine is served in a bistro-casual atmosphere by attentive servers. Portions are a good size but not enormous, and the kitchen's attention to detail is impressive. The wine list features all sorts of Mendocino County vintages, plus a good range of European wines. Most wines are available by the bottle only, but the servers will gladly cork an unfinished bottle so you can take it home to enjoy later.

Information and Services

If you need assistance with local lodging, dining, or wine-tasting, try the visitors center at the **Ukiah Valley Conference Center** (200 S. School St., 707/463-6700). Since Ukiah is the county seat, you can find information here about both the city of Ukiah and Mendocino County.

For local flavor, pick up a copy of the *Ukiah Daily Journal* (www.ukiahdailyjournal.com) for the best in up-to-date entertainment and events.

The **Ukiah Valley Medical Center** (275 Hospital Dr., 707/462-3111, www.uvmc.org) has a 24-hour emergency room as part of its full-service facility.

Ukiah has branches of many major banks. You can also find a **post office** (617 S. Orchard Ave., 707/462-3231, www.usps.com). Internet access is available, often for a fee, at many of the chain motels and, of course, at the various Starbucks and other cafés.

Getting There and Around

Ukiah is about 110 miles north of San Francisco (2 hours), a straight shot on U.S. 101. It's also about 60 miles north of Santa Rosa (1 hour) on U.S. 101. From Eureka (3 hours away), take U.S. 101 south for 157 miles. To get to Ukiah from Sacramento (under 3 hours), take I-5 north for 58 miles to exit 578 in Williams, and then get on Highway 20 west. After 79 miles, turn south on U.S. 101 to reach Ukiah in another 6.6 miles.

The **Mendocino Transit Authority** (800/696-4682, www.4mta.org) runs bus service throughout the county, with Ukiah as the hub; you can catch buses here and in Mendocino and Fort Bragg. Private pilots can land at **Ukiah Municipal Airport** (UKI, 1411 S. State St., 707/467-2817, www.cityofukiah.com).

The Redwood Coast

Of all the natural wonders California has to offer, the one that seems to inspire the purest and most unmitigated awe is the giant redwood. *Sequoia sempervirens,* also called coast redwood, grows along the California coast from around Big Sur in the south and into southern Oregon in the north. Coast redwoods hold the records for the tallest trees ever recorded, and are among the world's oldest and all-around most massive living things. The two best places to experience extensive wild groves of these gargantuan treasures are Humboldt Redwoods State Park, in Humboldt County, and Redwood National and State Parks, near the north end of California around Eureka and Crescent City.

Most of the major park areas along the Redwood Coast can be accessed via U.S. 101 and U.S. 199. Follow the signs to the smaller roads that lead farther from civilization. To get to the redwood parks from the south, drive up U.S. 101 or the much slower but prettier Highway 1. The two roads merge at Leggett, north of Fort Bragg, and continue north as U.S. 101.

People camping in the parks usually pack in their own food and cook at their campsites. To restock, you can drive to Crescent City to find a market or to Eureka for a true supermarket.

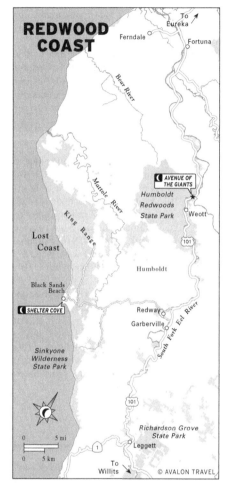

REDWOOD COAST

To Eureka

Ferndale

Fortuna

Bear River

AVENUE OF THE GIANTS

Humboldt Redwoods State Park

Weott

Mattole River

King Range

101

Lost Coast

Humboldt

Black Sands Beach

SHELTER COVE

Redway

Garberville

South Fork Eel River

Sinkyone Wilderness State Park

101

Richardson Grove State Park

0   5 mi

0   5 km

Leggett

To Willits

© AVALON TRAVEL

LEGGETT

As Highway 1 heads inland toward Leggett, the ocean views are replaced with redwoods. This part of the road is curvy, winding, and sun-dappled. It's a beautiful drive, so take it slow.

At the junction of Highway 1 and U.S. 101, you'll enter Leggett, famed for the local attraction **Chandelier Drive-Thru Tree** (67402 Drive-Thru Tree Rd., 707/925-6464, www. drivethrutree.com, daily dawn-dusk, $5). The

tree opening is about six feet wide and a little over six feet high. Kids will be thrilled. And, of course, there's a gift shop.

You might slow down as you approach **The Peg House** (69501 U.S. 101, 707/925-6444, http://thepeghouse.net) because of the fake police car situated by the highway. But there's another reason to ease off the gas at this general store and gas station. Believe it or not, The Peg House, which was built with pegs not nails, gets raves for its burgers, tri-tip, and deli sandwiches. Sometimes there is even live music.

GARBERVILLE AND REDWAY

Garberville is the first real town in Humboldt County. Located just three miles northwest is the slightly larger town of Redway, with just a few hundred more residents than Garberville. Known as the "Gateway to the Avenue of the Giants," the two towns can also be considered the gateway to the Lost Coast, since the biggest community along that remote coastline, Shelter Cove, is accessible via a winding 23-mile road from Redway. (Shelter Cove is also the southern terminus of the Lost Coast Trail.) Both towns are good places to get a meal or fill your tank with gas before heading west to the coast or north to the redwoods.

As U.S. 101 continues north, logging trucks hauling massive slabs of lumber become more prevalent, and the roadsides are punctuated with dreadlocked hitchhikers trying to bum a ride.

Richardson Grove State Park

Even if your main destination is a redwood park farther north, save time for a stop at **Richardson Grove State Park** (1600 U.S. 101, 707/247-3318, www.parks.ca.gov, $8), the first of the old-growth redwoods along U.S. 101. This park has special features all its own, like a tree you can walk through and the ninth-tallest coast redwood. The Eel River flows through the park, offering good fishing as well as camping, swimming, and hiking. The visitors center (May-Sept.) in the 1930s Richardson Grove Lodge has cool exhibits and a nature store. Richardson Grove State Park is seven miles south of Garberville.

Mateel Community Center

Located in Redway, the **Mateel Community Center** (59 Rusk Ln., Redway, 707/923-3368, www.mateel.org) brings music, theater, dance, comedy, film, and craft events to southern Humboldt. They also put on local annual events, including Reggae on the River, the Humboldt Hills Hoedown, and the Halloween Boogie. Check the website for a full list of upcoming events.

Accommodations

The place to stay is the **C Benbow Inn** (445 Lake Benbow Dr., 707/923-2124 or 800/355-3301, www.benbowinn.com, $99-575). A swank resort backing onto Lake Benbow, this inn has it all: a gourmet restaurant, a nine-hole golf course, an outdoor swimming pool, and a woodsy atmosphere that blends perfectly with the ancient redwood forest surrounding it. Guest rooms glow with dark polished woods and jewel-toned carpets. Wide king and comfy queen beds beckon guests tired after a long day of hiking in the redwoods or golfing beside the inn.

Several small motels offer reasonable guest rooms, and many have outdoor pools where weary guests can cool off during the heat of summer. The best of these is the **Best Western Humboldt House Inn** (701 Redwood Dr., 707/923-2771, www.bestwestern.com, $140-200). Guest rooms are clean and comfortable, the pool is sparkling and cool, the breakfast is hot, and the location is convenient to restaurants and shops in Garberville. Expect the usual comforts of the Best Western chain. Most guest rooms have two queen beds, great for families and pairs of couples traveling together on a budget.

Camping

Richardson Grove State Park (1600 U.S. 101, 800/444-7275, www.parks.ca.gov, camping $35) has 169 campsites in three campground areas surrounded by redwoods and the Elk River.

You can park your RV year-round at the 112 sites of the posh **Benbow RV Park** (7000 Benbow Dr., 707/923-2777 or 866/236-2697, www.benbowrv.com, $52-60). Premium sites come with complimentary tea and scones at the nearby Benbow Inn.

Food

The restaurant at the **C Benbow Inn** (445 Lake Benbow Dr., 707/923-2124 or 800/355-3301, www.benbowinn.com, daily breakfast, lunch, and dinner, $19-45) matches the lodgings for superiority in the area. It serves upscale California cuisine, with a vegan menu available on request, and features an extensive wine list with many regional wineries represented. The white-tablecloth dining room is exquisite, and the expansive outdoor patio overlooking the water is the perfect place to sit as the temperature cools on a summer evening.

Garberville has several modest eateries that appeal to weary travelers and families with kids. One of these is the **Woodrose Café** (911 Redwood Dr., 707/923-3191, www.woodrosecafe.com, Mon.-Fri. 8am-2pm, Sat.-Sun. 8am-1pm, $9-14). You can get a traditional American-style breakfast and lunch at this small independent eatery, and a lot of the food is organic, local, and healthy, but it doesn't come cheap.

Another good breakfast and lunch stop is the **Eel River Café** (801 Redwood Dr., 707/923-3783, Tues.-Sat. 6am-2pm, $6-12), a diner all the way with black and white checkerboard floors and a long counter with red stools. Try the chicken fried steak with biscuits and gravy.

Need a pick-me-up? You won't find too many Starbucks around here, so enjoy a taste of local Humboldt-roasted coffee instead in Redway. The **Signature Coffee** (3455 Redwood Dr., Redway, 707/923-2661, www.signaturecoffeecompany.com, Mon.-Fri. 7am-5pm) takes pride in its organic product and sustainable practices, and they sell bagged coffee too, so you can stock up for use at the campsite.

There's a supermarket in Garberville, **Ray's Food Place** (875 Redwood Dr., 707/923-2279, www.gorays.com, daily 7am-10pm).

Information and Services

The **Garberville Redway Area Chamber of Commerce** (782 Redwood Dr., 800/923-2613, www.garberville.org, Labor Day-Memorial Day Mon.-Fri. 9am-4pm, Memorial Day-Labor Day Mon.-Fri. 9am-4pm, Sat.-Sun. 10am-4pm) is happy to help visitors get acquainted with the area. There is a convenient **post office** (3400 Redwood Dr., Redway, 707/923-3784, www.usps.com, Mon.-Fri. 8:45am-4:45pm) in nearby Redway. The nearest hospital with an emergency room is **Redwood Memorial Hospital** (3300 Renner Dr., Fortuna, 707/725-3361, www.redwoodmemorial.org).

Getting There and Around

Garberville is located 65 miles south of Eureka and 200 miles north of San Francisco on U.S. 101. From Garberville, take Redwood Drive just three miles to Redway. The best way to get to Humboldt Redwoods State Park from either direction is via U.S. 101. You can also approach the center of the park from Mattole Road from the Lost Coast (Shelter Cove to Mattole). Road signs point to the Avenue of the Giants. Bicycles are not permitted on U.S. 101, but you can ride the Avenue of the Giants and Mattole Road.

The little towns of the Humboldt redwoods region can be short on necessary services such as gas stations. There is a **76 Gas Station** (790 Redwood Dr.) well off the highway.

The **Redwood County Transit** (707/464-6400, www.redwoodtransit.org) bus system offers limited service to Garberville from the north.

HUMBOLDT REDWOODS STATE PARK

Surprisingly, the largest stand of unlogged redwood trees isn't on the coast, and it isn't in the Sierras; it's here in Humboldt, bisected by U.S. 101. Come to this park to hike beneath 300-foot-plus old-growth trees that began their lives centuries before Europeans knew California existed. One highlight of the park is the 10,000-acre Rockefeller Forest, the largest contiguous old growth redwood

forest in the world. Start your visit at the **Humboldt Redwoods State Park Visitors Center** (707/946-2263, www.parks.ca.gov or www.humboldtredwoods.org, Apr.-Oct. daily 9am-5pm, Nov.-Mar. daily 10am-4pm), located along the Avenue of the Giants (Hwy. 254), between the towns of Weott and Myers Flat. It's a nice visitors center, with plenty of information for anyone new to the region or looking for hiking or camping information. You can also enjoy the theater, interpretive museum and gift shop. There is no entrance fee for Humboldt Redwoods State Park and no fee to use the visitors center; the only day-use fee in the park is for the Williams Grove Day Use Area ($8 per vehicle).

While it's more than worth your while to spend a weekend or more in the Humboldt redwoods, you can also enjoy yourself for a few hours just passing through. A drive along the Avenue of the Giants with a stop at the visitors center and a quick nature walk or picnic can give you a quick taste of the lovely southern end of the coastal redwoods region.

◖ Avenue of the Giants

The most famous stretch of redwood trees is the **Avenue of the Giants** (www.avenueofthe-giants.net), paralleling U.S. 101 and the Eel River for about 33 miles between Garberville and Fortuna; look for signs on U.S. 101. Visitors come from all over the world to drive this stretch of road and gaze in wonder at the sky-high old-growth redwoods along the way. Campgrounds and hiking trails sprout among the trees off the road. Park your car at various points along the way and get out to walk among the giants. Or walk down to the nearby Eel River for a cool dip.

The Avenue's highest traffic volume is in July-August, when you can expect bumper-to-bumper stop-and-go traffic along the entire road. That's not necessarily a bad thing, as going slow is the best way to see the sights. But if crowds aren't your thing, you might try visiting in spring or fall, or even braving the rains of winter to gain a more secluded redwood experience.

© STUART THORNTON

a drive down the Avenue of the Giants

To enhance your Avenue of the Giants drive, there's an eight-stop audio tour along the route. Pick up an audio tour card at the visitors center or on either side of the drive.

Hiking and Biking

Stop at the Humboldt Redwoods State Park Visitors Center (707/946-2263, www.parks.ca.gov or www.humboldtredwoods.org, Apr.-Oct. daily 9am-5pm, Nov.-Mar. daily 10am-4pm) to pick up a trail map showing the number of hikes accessible on or near this road. Many are very short, so you can make a nice day of combined driving and walking without having to commit to one big trek.

Many visitors start with the **Founder's Grove Nature Loop Trail** (0.6 miles, easy), at mile marker 20.5 on the Avenue of the Giants. This sedate, flat nature trail gives walkers a taste of the big old-growth trees in the park. Sadly, the onetime tallest tree in the world, the Dyerville Giant, fell in 1991 at the age of about 1,600. But it's still doing its part in this astounding ecosystem, decomposing before your eyes on the forest floor and feeding new life in the forest.

Right at the visitors center, you can enjoy the **Gould Grove Nature Trail** (0.6 miles, easy)—a wheelchair-accessible interpretive nature walk with helpful signs describing the denizens of the forest.

If you're looking for a longer walk in the woods, try the lovely **River Trail** (Mattole Rd., 1.1 miles west of Ave. of the Giants, 7 miles round-trip, moderate). It follows the South Fork Eel River, allowing access to yet another ecosystem. Check with the visitors center to be sure that the summer bridges have been installed before trying to hike this trail.

Hard-core hikers who like to go at it all day can get their exercise at Humboldt Redwoods State Park. Start at the **Grasshopper Multiuse Trailhead** (Mattole Rd., 5.1 miles west of Ave. of the Giants) to access the newer **Johnson Camp Trail** (10.5 miles round-trip, difficult) that takes you to the abandoned cabins of railroad tie makers. Or pick another fork from the same trailhead to climb more than 3,000 feet to **Grasshopper Peak** (13.5 miles, difficult). From the peak, you can see 100 miles in any direction, overlooking the whole of the park and beyond.

You can bring your street bike to the park and ride the Avenue of the Giants or Mattole Road. A number of the trails around Humboldt Redwoods State Park are designated multiuse, which means that mountain bikers can make the rigorous climbs and then rip their way back down.

Swimming and Kayaking

The **Eel River**'s forks meander through the Humboldt redwoods, creating lots of great opportunities for cooling off on hot summer days. Check with the park's visitors center for this year's best swimming holes, but you can reliably find good spots at **Eagle Point,** near Hidden Valley Campground; **Gould Bar;** and **Garden Club of America Grove.** In addition to the usual precautions for river swimming, during August-September a poisonous (if ingested) blue-green algae can bloom late in the summer, making swimming in certain parts of the river hazardous.

Events

Humboldt Redwoods State Park is the site of a couple of the best marathons and half-marathons around. It offers flat courses, cool weather, and world-class scenery. If you're looking for an unintimidating place to try your first marathon, or if you need a fast time for a personal record to qualify for Boston, this is an ideal choice. These events are also less crowded than the famous marathons, and you can camp right in the park where they begin. October has the **Humboldt Redwoods Marathon** (www. redwoodsmarathon.org, $55-65) with a related half-marathon ($50-60) and a 5K ($25). The **Avenue of the Giants Marathon** (www.theave. org, marathon $60, half-marathon $50, 10K $30) is held each May.

Camping

There are few lodging options close to the park. Fortunately, the camping at Humboldt

Redwoods State Park (707/946-2263, www. reserveamerica.com, $35) is good, with three developed car-accessible campgrounds; there are also primitive backcountry campsites ($5). Each developed campground has its own entrance station, and reservations are strongly recommended, as the park is quite popular with weekend campers.

Burlington Campground (707/946-1811, year-round) is adjacent to the visitors center and is a convenient starting point for the marathons and other races that traverse the park in May and October. It's dark and comfortable, engulfed in trees, and has ample restroom facilities and hot showers. **Albee Creek** (Mattole Rd., 5 miles west of Ave. of the Giants, 707/946-2472, mid-May-mid-Oct.) offers some redwood-shaded sites and others in open meadows, which can be nice in the summer if you want to get a little sun. **◖ Hidden Springs Campground** (Ave. of the Giants, 5 miles south of the visitors center, 707/943-3177, early May-Labor Day) is large and popular. Nearby a trail leads to a great Eel River swimming hole. Minimalist campers will enjoy the seclusion of hike-in trail camps at **Johnson** and **Grasshopper Peak.**

Equestrians can also make use of the multiuse trails, and the **Cuneo Creek Horse Camp** (old homestead on Mattole Rd., 8 miles west of Ave. of the Giants, May-mid-Oct., 1 vehicle and 2 horses $35) provides a place for riders who want to spend more than just a day exploring the thousands of acres of forest and meadowland.

Information and Services

Get the best information at the **Humboldt Redwoods State Park Visitors Center** (707/946-2263, www.parks.ca.gov or www. humboldtredwoods.org, Apr.-Oct. daily 9am-5pm, Nov.-Mar. daily 10am-4pm). You can fill your car up in the nearby towns of Piercy, Garberville, Redway, Redcrest, Miranda, and Rio Dell. Markets to stock up on supplies are in Garberville, Redway, Miranda, Phillipsville, Redcrest, Myers Flat, Scotia, and Rio Dell. The nearest hospital with an emergency room is **Redwood Memorial Hospital** (3300 Renner Dr., Fortuna, 707/725-3361, www.redwood-memorial.org).

Getting There

Humboldt Redwoods State Park is 21 miles north of Garberville on U.S. 101. The Avenue of the Giants parallels U.S. 101 and there are several marked exits along the highway to reach the scenic redwood drive.

FERNDALE

Ferndale was built in the 19th century by Scandinavian immigrants who came to California to farm. Little has changed since the immigrants constructed their fanciful ginger-bread Victorian homes and shops. Many cows still munch grass in the dairy pastures that surround the town today.

The main sight in Ferndale is the town itself, which has been designated a historical landmark. Ferndale is all Victorian, all the time: Ask about the building you're in and you'll be told all about its specific architectural style, its construction date, and its original occupants. Main Street's shops, galleries, inns, and restaurants are all set into scrupulously maintained and restored late-19th-century buildings, and even the public restrooms are housed in a small Victorianesque structure.

Architecture buffs can spend hours just strolling around downtown. So it's no surprise that Hollywood has discovered Ferndale as a picturesque setting for a movie: it has starred alongside Jim Carrey in *The Majestic* and Dustin Hoffman in *Outbreak*.

Sights

The **Ferndale History Museum** (515 Shaw St., 707/786-4466, www.ferndale-museum.org, June-Sept. Tues.-Sat. 11am-4pm, Sun. 1pm-4pm, Oct.-Dec. and Feb.-May Wed.-Sat. 11am-4pm, Sun. 1pm-4pm, $1) is a block off Main Street and tells the story of the town. Life-size dioramas depict period life in a Victorian home, and an array of antique artifacts brings history to life. Downstairs, the implements of rural coast history vividly display

the reality that farmers and artisans faced in the preindustrial era.

To cruise farther back into the town's history, consider wandering out into the **Ferndale Cemetery** on Bluff Street. Well-tended tombstones and mausoleums wend up the hillside behind the town. Genealogists will love reading the scrupulously maintained epitaphs that tell the human history of the region.

Beaches

Ferndale locals love that they have their own beach just five miles outside of their quaint village. The **Centerville County Park and Beach** (five miles west of Ferndale on Centerville Rd., 707/445-7651, http://co.humboldt.ca.us, daily 5am-midnight, free) stretches for an impressive nine miles and is home to a winter congregation of tundra swans. You are able to drive your four-wheel drive on the sand, ride a horse, or build a big beach bonfire at night here, which is unusual for beaches in California.

Entertainment and Events

Ferndale is a quiet town where the sidewalks roll up early. But for visitors who like to be out and about after 6pm, there are a few decent options. The **Ferndale Repertory Theater** (447 Main St., 707/786-5483 or 800/838-3006, www.ferndale-rep.org, $13-18), the oldest and largest of the North Coast's community theaters, puts on a number of shows each year. Some are wholesome and suitable for the whole family like *Annie*, while others, including *In the Next Room (Or the Vibrator Play)*, feature more adult subject matter. Be sure to check what's on when you're in town. Also check the schedule for special events and performances.

If you want to get a beer or mixed drink in Ferndale, **The Palace** (353 Main St., 707/786-4165, daily 10am-2am) is the local bar with pool tables, shuffleboard, and a jukebox. Late into the night, you can fill the slots at the **Bear River Casino** (11 Bear Paws Way, Loleta, 707/733-9644, www.bearrivercasino.com, daily open 24 hours) in nearby Loleta.

Ferndale has hosted the **Humboldt County Fair** (1250 5th St., www.humboldtcountyfair.

org, adults $8, seniors and students under $8) each August since 1896. For 10 days people from all around the county come to celebrate at the old-fashioned fair, complete with livestock exhibits and horse racing, competitions, a carnival, musical entertainment each night, and a variety of shows for kids and adults on the fairground stages. If you're in the area, come join the fun.

The **Kinetic Sculpture Museum** (580 Main St., 707/733-3841, usually daily 10am-5pm) salutes wacky modernity in all its colorful, weird glory. As the end point of the annual Kinetic Grand Championship sculpture race (www.kineticgrandchampionship.com), Ferndale has the honor of housing a number of these sculptures. The museum is a repository of more than 40 years' worth of artifacts from the great race; docents do not interpret the art, so visitors are free to make what they will of the duckies, froggies, airplanes, and bicycles.

Shopping

A tour of Ferndale's Main Street shops makes for an idyllic morning stroll. The Victorian storefronts house antiques stores, jewelry shops, clothing boutiques, and art galleries. Ferndale is also a surprisingly good place to buy a hat.

The **Golden Gait Mercantile** (421 Main St., 707/786-4891, Mon.-Sat. 10am-5pm) has it all: antiques, candies, gourmet foodstuffs, clothing, hats, souvenirs, and more. Antiques and collectibles tend to be small and reasonably priced. By comparison, **Silva's Fine Jewelry** (400 Ocean Ave., 707/786-4425, www.silvasjewelry.com, daily 8:30am-9pm), on the bottom floor of the Victorian Inn, is not a place for the faint of wallet. But the jewels, both contemporary and antique, are classically gorgeous. Another jewel is the **Blacksmith Shop** (455 Main St., 707/786-4216, www.ferndaleblacksmith.com, daily 9:30am-5:30pm) which displays a striking collection of useful art made by top blacksmiths and glassblowers from around the country. The array of jewelry, furniture, kitchen implements, fireplace tools, and metal things defies description. A gentler warmth comes from the **Golden Bee Candleworks** (451 Main St., 707/786-4508, Wed.-Sat. 10am-5pm, Sun. 11am-4pm),

purveyor of fine products made with honey and beeswax. The candles, soaps, and much more make the whole store smell delicious.

Accommodations

In Ferndale, lodgings tend to be, of course, Victorian-style inns, mostly bed-and-breakfasts. Guests of the **Shaw House Inn** (703 Main St., 707/786-9958 or 800/557-7429, www.shawhouse.com, $125-275) must walk a block or two to get to the heart of downtown Ferndale, but the reward for staying outside the town center is a spacious garden worth a stroll. In the heat of the afternoon, huge shade trees and perfectly positioned garden benches make a lovely spot to sit and read a book, hold a quiet conversation, or just enjoy the serene beauty of garden and town. The interior of the Shaw House has eight guest rooms and three common parlor areas. A lush morning breakfast fortifies shoppers ready to walk up and down Main Street and adventurers preparing to head to the deserted beaches of the Lost Coast or the trails in the nearby redwood forests.

The ◖ **Victorian Inn** (400 Ocean Ave., 707/786-4949 or 888/589-1808, www.victorianvillageinn.com, $115-259) is an imposing structure at the corner of Ocean Avenue and Main Street that also houses Silva's Jewelry. The inn comprises 13 guest rooms, all decorated with antique furnishings, luxurious linens, and pretty knickknacks. For a special treat, rent the Ira Russ Suite, a spacious room with a tower alcove that takes in the town below. In the mornings, a full hot breakfast is served to guests in the downstairs of this historic hotel.

Nothing in Ferndale is far from anything else in Ferndale, and **Hotel Ivanhoe** (315 Main St., 707/786-9000, www.ivanhoe-hotel.com, $95-145) is kitty-corner across from the Victorian Inn. In a town full of history, the Ivanhoe is the oldest extant hostelry. Plaques on the building's exterior describe its rich legacy. Fully refurbished in the 1990s, the four guest rooms are done in rich colors that revive the Western Victorian atmosphere of the original hotel.

If bric-a-brac and scented soaps make your skin itch, an inexpensive not-an-inn lodging

© STUART THORNTON

Ferndale's Victorian Inn

option in Ferndale is the **Redwood Suites** (332 Ocean Ave., 707/786-5000 or 888/589-1863, www.redwoodsuites.com, $95-145). Only a block off Main Street, the property has modern guest rooms that are simple but comfortable. Family suites with full kitchens are available, and the room rates are reasonable.

Food

Tucked into the bottom floor of the Victorian Inn, the **VI Restaurant & Tavern** (400 Ocean Ave., 707/786-4950, http://virestaurant. com, daily 11:30am-9pm, $10-36) feels like a spruced-up Western saloon. Perch yourself at the bar for casual options like fish and chips or sit down at a table for sophisticated dinner entrées like Portuguese paella or antelope short ribs.

Locals come from as far away as Eureka to dine at the restaurant at the **Hotel Ivanhoe** (315 Main St., 707/786-9000, www.ivanhoe-hotel.com, Wed.-Sun. 5pm-9pm, Wed.-Sun. bar from 4pm, $12-23). It's all about the hearty homemade Italian dishes and friendly personal service. A more casual Italian dining experience can be had down the street at the **Ferndale Pizza Co.** (607 Main St., 707/786-4345, Tues.-Thurs. 11:30am-9pm, Fri.-Sat. 11:30am-9:30pm, Sun. noon-9pm, $16-21).

If your accommodations don't include breakfast, stop in at the local favorite **Poppa Joe's** (409 Main St., 707/786-4180, Mon.-Fri. 6am-2pm, Sat.-Sun. 6am-noon, $5.50-9). The interior is dim and narrow, but the breakfast and lunch offerings are delicious.

If you need to grab some grub to go, **Valley Grocery** (339 Main St., 707/786-9515, daily 7am-10pm) stocks staples and also maintains a deli; it's a perfect last stop on the way out to a beach picnic. Don't forget to stop at the heavenly candy store **Sweetness and Light** (554 Main St., 707/786-4403 or 800/547-8180, www.sweetnessandlight.com, Mon.-Sat. 10am-5pm, Sun. 11am-4pm).

Information and Services

The *Ferndale Enterprise* (707/786-4611, www.ferndaleenterprise.us, $1) is published once a week on Thursday. The paper also puts out a free souvenir edition once a year just for visitors. Many inns and shops carry the souvenir edition all year long.

If you need medical care, the **Humboldt Medical Group** (528 Washington St., 707/786-4028, www.humboldtmedicalgroup.com) can assist you. Ferndale has a **post office** (536 Main St., 707/786-4642, www.usps.com, Mon.-Fri. 8:30am-5pm, Sat. 10am-noon).

Getting There and Around

Ferndale, like much of the nearby Lost Coast, is not directly accessible from U.S. 101; from U.S. 101 at Fernbridge, follow Highway 211 to Ferndale. Mattole Road leads out of town south toward the Sinkyone Wilderness area, while Centerville Road heads out to the beach. Walking provides the best views and feel of the town.

The Lost Coast

The Lost Coast is one of California's true last undeveloped coastlines. Encompassing northern Mendocino County and southern Humboldt County, this coast is "lost" because the rugged terrain makes it impractical—some might say impossible—to build a highway here. An arduous trek along its wilderness trails is worthwhile to soak up the raw beauty of its rugged beaches.

The King Range National Conservation Area encompasses the northern section of the Lost Coast. Here, King's Peak rises over 4,000 feet from the sea in less than three miles. It's also home to the most popular version of the Lost Coast Trail: a 24-mile backpacking excursion along the region's wild beaches that begins at the mouth of the Mattole River and ends at Shelter Cove's Black Sand Beach.

The Sinkyone Wilderness State Park makes up the southern section of the Lost Coast, which has its own Lost Coast Trail, heading slightly inland on its journey from Bear Harbor to Usal Beach. While the more popular King Range Lost Coast Trail traverses beaches right by the ocean, the 16-mile Sinkyone version is mostly along bluffs with less coastal access.

Situated between the two major sections of the King Range Conservation Area and the Sinkyone Wilderness State Park is the small fishing community of Shelter Cove, which has a few restaurant and lodging options. It's also home to Black Sand Beach and the Cape Mendocino Lighthouse. The few other areas of the Lost Coast accessible by car include Usal Beach and Mattole Beach.

Reaching the Lost Coast involves short detours from U.S. 101. Shelter Cove can be reached by taking Briceland/Shelter Cove Road out of Redway, while Usal Beach is accessible from a dirt road that leaves Highway 1 three miles north of the town of Rockport. The Mattole Recreation Site is found by taking Lighthouse Road off Mattole Road.

MATTOLE ROAD

Mattole Road, a narrow, mostly paved two-lane road, affords views of remote ranchland, unspoiled forests, and a few short miles of barely accessible cliffs and beaches. It's one of the few paved drivable routes that allows you to view the Lost Coast from your car (the other is Shelter Cove Road, farther south). In sunny weather, the vistas are spectacular. This road also serves as access to the even smaller tracks out to the trails and campgrounds of the Sinkyone Wilderness. The most common way to get to Mattole Road is from the Victorian village of Ferndale, where you take a right on Ocean Avenue and follow the signs towards the community of Petrolia.

MATTOLE BEACH

At the northern end of the Lost Coast, **Mattole Beach** (end of Lighthouse Rd., 707/825-2300, www.publiclands.org) is a broad length of sand that's perfect for an easy contemplative stroll. It's also popular for picnicking and fishing. Mattole Beach is also the northern entry point to the Lost Coast Trail, and the start of

LOST COAST

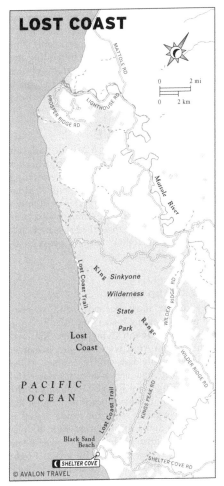

0   2 mi
0   2 km

PACIFIC
OCEAN

© AVALON TRAVEL

THE LOST COAST TRAIL

To fully experience one of the country's most remote and rugged coastal areas, backpackers head out on the **Lost Coast Trail.** This 24-mile beach hike stretches from the Mattole River down to Shelter Cove's Black Sand Beach. This is a once-in-a-lifetime experience, hiking alongside primal, mostly wild coastline, interrupted only by the abandoned Punta Gorda Lighthouse and numerous shipwrecks along shore. Waterfalls feather the coastal bluffs, shorebirds fly above the crashing surf, sea lions congregate at the aptly named Sea Lion Gulch, and migrating whales surface along the horizon. On land, you might encounter deer and bears.

This is a strenuous hike, challenging even for experienced hikers. It demands both preparation and stamina. While scenic, the ocean along the trail is also cold, rough, and unforgiving. Use caution, as multiple people have been swept out to sea.

Planning Your Hike

You can hike the trail anytime between spring and fall. Spring is notable for blooming wildflowers. Summer is the most crowded. Fall is the least crowded, and often has the most pleasant weather. During winter, the trail can be impassable due to massive surf or flooding streams.

Allow three days and two nights to complete the trail, hiking around eight miles a day. Be prepared to walk on sand, cobblestones, and boulders. Plan on carrying in everything you'll need (tents, sleeping bags, equipment, food, and water). Carry it all (including any trash) back out to keep the area wild. There are creeks every 1.5-2 miles along the trail, but you need to purify the water before drinking it.

Most people begin the hike at the Mattole River and head south. This is so you are hiking with the winds at your back, rather than in your face. You'll need to park a vehicle at either end of the trail. Parking at the Mattole trailhead is free. There have been vehicle break-ins, so don't leave any valuables in your car. Parking at Black Sand Beach, the southern end of the

a shorter, six-mile round-trip day hike to the **Punta Gorda Lighthouse.** The lighthouse was built in 1911 after the coast and its rocks caused multiple shipwrecks. It was shut down in 1951 due to high maintenance costs.

To reach Mattole Beach from U.S. 101, take the Garberville, Honeydew, or Ferndale exits. Follow the signs to Petrolia on Mattole Road. Turn off Mattole Road onto Lighthouse Road, which is south of the Mattole River Bridge. Follow Lighthouse Road for five miles to the beach.

trail, is also free. The drive between the two trailheads is an hour and 45 minutes. To avoid a half-day of driving between the trailheads, contact **Lost Coast Shuttle** (707/986-7437, www.lostcoastshuttle.com, $200/two people, $25/each additional person), which will drive you from Shelter Cove's Black Sand Beach, where you can leave your car, to the start of the trailhead at Mattole Beach.

In addition to securing transportation, hikers also need a backcountry permit, but these are free as long as you're not an organized group or a commercial enterprise. They also double as fire permits. You can get a permit at a self-service box at one of the trailheads, at the **King Range office** in Whitethorn, or at the **field office** in Arcata (707/986-5400, www.ca.blm. gov/arcata/kingrange).

Bear canisters are mandatory for storing your food and scented items while on the trail so that your camp doesn't attract bears. You can rent bear canisters ($5) just a few miles from the Mattole Trailhead at the **Petrolia General Store** (40 Sherman Rd., Petrolia, 707/629-3455). They're also available in Shelter Cove at **BLM Whitethorn Office** (768 Shelter Cove Rd., 707/986-5400, $5) or in Arcata at the **BLM Arcata Field Office** (1695 Heindon Rd., 707/825-2300, $5).

This is a wilderness hike so there are few signs. You'll mostly just be hiking the beach except for a few spots. Two sections of the trail are impassable at high tides. The first is from Sea Lion Gulch to Randall Creek. The second is from south of Big Flat down to Gitchell Creek. So it's critical to consult a tide chart and manage your time to make sure you pass through these areas of the trail during low tide.

There are no developed campgrounds or facilities along the trail, but dispersed camping is allowed at **Cooksie Creek, Randall Creek, Big Creek, Big Flat Creek, Buck Creek, Shipman Creek** and **Gitchell Creek.**

Dogs are allowed on the trail as long as they are under voice control or on a leash. Dogs should be outfitted with booties so that their paws don't get scraped up by the rocks on the trail.

Before heading to the area, try to get your hands on a copy of Wilderness Press' **Lost Coast Map** (www.wildernesspress.com). You can check on trail conditions by visiting the **U.S. Department of the Interior** website: www.blm.gov/ca (search on "Lost Coast Trail"). More information is also available at the **King Range Information Line** (707/825-2300).

◖ SHELTER COVE

If you're not up for hiking a 24-mile trail, you can still get a taste of the Lost Coast in Shelter Cove, a fishing community with a scattering of restaurants and accommodations. A nine-hole golf course, a small airport, and 40 miles of paved roads and lots are remnants of a large planned community that failed to materialize. But the real highlight of Shelter Cove is its access to the shoreline.

Sights
BLACK SAND BEACH
One of the most beautiful and accessible features of the Lost Coast, the 3.5 mile **Black Sand Beach** (King Range National Conservation Area, www.blm.gov) is named for its unusually dark sand and stones, which contrast with the deep blue ocean water and the towering King Range Mountains in the background. The main beach parking lot has interpretive panels about the region as well as bathrooms and a drinking fountain. It's just north of the town of Shelter Cove; to get there follow Shelter Cove Road, then take a right onto Beach Road, which dead-ends at Black Sand Beach. The long walk across the dark sands to either Horse Creek or Gitchell Creek is relatively easy. This beach also serves as the south end of the Lost Coast Trail.

CAPE MENDOCINO LIGHTHOUSE
At Mal Coombs Park in Shelter Cove, the 43-foot tower of the **Cape Mendocino Lighthouse** (www.lighthousefriends.com, tours Memorial Day-Labor Day daily 10:30am-3:30pm) is quiet and dark. It began life on Cape Mendocino—a 400-foot cliff that marks the westernmost point of California—in 1868. In 1951 the tower was

abandoned in favor of a light on a pole, and in 1999 the tower was moved to Shelter Cove, becoming a museum in 2000. When docents are available, you can take a tour of the lighthouse. The original first-order Fresnel lens is now on display in nearby Ferndale.

Sports and Recreation

HIKING

For another great hike, take the **King Crest Trail,** a mountain hike from the southern Saddle Mountain Trailhead to stunning King Peak and on to the North Slide Peak Trailhead. A good solid 10-mile one-day round-trip can be done from either trailhead. To reach Saddle Mountain Trailhead from Shelter Cove, drive up Shelter Cove Road and turn left onto King Peak Road. Bear left on Saddle Mountain Road and turn left on a spur road to the trailhead. Note that only high clearance, four-wheel drive vehicles are recommended.

Also accessible from the Saddle Mountain Trailhead, **Buck Creek Trail** includes an infamous grade, descending more than 3,000 vertical feet on an old logging road to the beach.

An arduous but gorgeous loop trail, the eight-mile **Hidden Valley-Chinquapin-Lost Coast Loop Trail** can be done in one day, or in two days with a stop at water-accessible Nick's Camp. Access it by driving out of Shelter Cove and turning right onto Chemise Mountain Road. The trailhead will be less than a mile on your right.

The many other trails in the Kings Range National Conservation Area near Shelter Cove include **Rattlesnake Ridge, Kinsey Ridge, Spanish Ridge,** and **Lightning.** Before heading to the area, try to get your hands on a copy of Wilderness Press' Lost Coast Map (www.wildernesspress.com).

FISHING

The Lost Coast is a natural fishing haven. The harbor at Shelter Cove offers charter services for ocean fishing. Kevin Riley of **Outcast Sportfishing** (Shelter Cove, 707/986-9842, www.outcastsportfish.com, Apr.-Sept., $225 pp per day) can help plan a charter fishing trip chasing whatever is in season. The cost includes gear, tackle, and filleting and packaging your fish at the end of the day, but bring your own lunch. Another reputable charter service is **Shelter Cove Sport Fishing** (707/923-1668, www.codking.com, fishing trips $150-225 pp), offering excursions to hunt halibut, albacore, salmon, or rockfish.

If shellfish is your favorite, come to the Shelter Cove area to enjoy the Northern California abalone season. Ask locally for this year's best diving spots, and be sure to obtain a license: The state Department of Fish and Game (888/773-8450, www.dfg.ca.gov) can explain the rules about taking abalone, which is strictly regulated.

SURFING

Big Flat is a legendary surf spot about eight miles north of Shelter Cove on the Lost Coast Trail. While the hike in is challenging, hard-core surfers will find it worth the effort. Local surfers are very protective of this break: Even a writer for *National Geographic Adventure* who wrote about the break, refused to name it for fear of retaliation. He referred to it as "Ghost Point." Be careful. Big Flat is in the middle of nowhere, and a surfer with a broken ankle in 2008 had to be airlifted out of the area.

Accommodations

Shelter Cove offers several nice motels for those who aren't up for roughing it in the wilderness overnight. At the **Shelter Cove Beachcomber Inn** (412 Machi Rd., 707/986-7551, $75-115), each guest room has its own character along with views of the coast or the woods. It's an easy stroll to the airstrip and harbor.

The Tides Inn of Shelter Cove (59 Surf Point, 707/986-7900 or 888/998-4337, www.sheltercovetidesinn.com, $165-215) has standard guest rooms as well as luxurious suites. The suites come with fireplaces and full kitchens. All of the guest rooms face the sea, only steps from the inn. The Tides Inn is centrally located within walking distance of the airstrip, local shops, and restaurants.

The **Inn of the Lost Coast** (205 Wave Dr., 707/986-7521 or 888/570-9676, www.innofthelostcoast.com, $150-250) has an array of large, airy guest rooms and suites with stellar views to suit even luxurious tastes. Ask about discounts for AOPA pilots and AARP members, as well as the AAA discount.

The **Cliff House at Shelter Cove** (141 Wave Dr., 707/986-7344, www.cliffhousesheltercove.com, $160-180) is perched atop the bluffs overlooking the black-sand beaches. Only two suites are available; they're perfect for a romantic vacation or family getaway. Each has a full kitchen, living room, bedroom, gas fireplace, and satellite TV.

Camping

For many, staying on the Lost Coast near Shelter Cove means camping in the wilderness near the trails. If you're planning to camp in the backcountry, you need a permit. Permits are free and can be obtained from self-service boxes at the trailheads, or by visiting the local office of the **Bureau of Land Management** (BLM, 768 Shelter Cove Rd., Whitethorn, 707/986-5400, www.ca.blm.gov). Bear canisters are mandatory; if you don't have one, you can rent one ($5) with a major credit card at the **Petrolia General Store** (40 Sherman Rd., Petrolia, 707/629-3455).

If you prefer a developed campground in the area around Shelter Cove with amenities like restrooms, grills, fire rings, picnic tables, bear boxes, and potable water, there are a number of sites in the King Range National Conservation Area (no permit required). Campgrounds are open year-round. Reservations are not available but the odds of getting a site are pretty good, given the small number of people who come here, even in high season. Some of the larger BLM camping areas (707/986-5400, www.ca.blm.gov) in the King Range are **Wailaki** (Chemise Mountain Rd., 13 sites, $8), **Nadelos** (Chemise Mountain Rd., tents only, 8 sites, $8), **Tolkan** (King Peak Rd., 5 RV sites, 4 tent sites, $8), and **Horse Mountain** (King Peak Rd., 9 sites, no water, $5). Trailers and RVs (up to 24 feet) are allowed at most sites except Nadelos.

If you are driving an RV, it's wise to check road conditions beforehand.

For more developed camping in Shelter Cove, the nearby **Shelter Cove RV Campground** (492 Machi Rd., Whitethorn, 707/986-7474, RVs $46, tents $36) is just feet away from the airport and has views of the ocean. They have a deli and store (summer daily 8am-6pm, winter daily 9am-5pm, grill summer daily 8am-5pm, winter daily 9am-4pm) on-site so you don't have to bring all your own food.

Food

For a delicious seafood meal, visit the glass-fronted A-frame **Chart Room** (210 Wave Dr., 707/986-9696, www.chartroom.cc, Sat.-Wed. 5pm-9pm, $20-25). Seafood and hearty meat and pasta dishes are available along with vegetarian fare, sandwiches, and soups. The Chart Room also has beer, wine, and cocktails that you can drink on the deck. Be sure to check out the nautical and aeronautical gift shop.

The hearty menu at the **Cove Restaurant** (10 Seal Ct., 707/986-1197, www.sheltercoveoceanfrontinn.com, Thurs.-Sun. 5pm-9pm, $13-30), heavy on the seafood, is perfect after a hard day of hiking, fishing, or beachcombing, especially with the Cove's views of the coast.

Enjoy a slice of pizza or a whole pie at **Fish Tank Pizzeria** (205 Wave Dr., 707/986-7672, Wed.-Sun. 4pm-9pm). Go for coffee, breakfast, or a sandwich at the **Fish Tank Espresso Gallery** (205 Wave Dr., 707/986-7850, Sun.-Thurs. 7am-2pm, Fri.-Sat. 7am-2pm and 5pm-9pm). The Espresso Gallery also serves sushi on Friday nights.

Information and Services

Don't expect much information or services in remote Shelter Cove. For an overview of the community, visit www.sheltercoveca.info and www.sheltercove-lostcoast.com. There's a **post office** (498 Shelter Cove Rd., Whitethorn, 707/986-7532, www.usps.com) on the road to Shelter Cove. There are no medical facilities in Shelter Cove, but emergency services are coordinated through the **Shelter Cove Fire Department** (9126 Shelter Cove Rd., region of steep coastal mountains and surf-pounded beaches spotted with wildlife, including bears and elk. The Roosevelt Elk had disappeared from the region until a herd from Prairie Creek State Park was reintroduced here. With their impressive antlers, the elk bulls usually weigh 700-1,100 pounds and can be quite a sight to see in the wild.

Though not as popular as the Lost Coast Trail connecting Black Sand Beach to the Mattole River up north, the Sinkyone Wilderness has a 16-mile **Lost Coast Trail** that starts at Bear Harbor, south of Needle Rock, and ends at Usal Beach. This trail, which takes backpackers 2-3 days, has more climbing than the more popular beach trail to the north. The rigorous hike is mostly on bluffs above the coastline. It passes through virgin redwood groves and mixed forest with beach access at **Wheeler Beach.**

wild Usal Beach

© STUART THORNTON

Whitethorn, 707/986-7507, www.sheltercove-ca.gov). The nearest hospital with an emergency room is **Redwood Memorial Hospital** (3300 Renner Dr., Fortuna, 707/725-3361, www.redwoodmemorial.org).

Getting There and Around

To reach Shelter Cove from U.S. 101 North, take the second Garberville exit. After exiting, look for the Shelter Cove signs and turn west on Briceland Road, which becomes Shelter Cove Road. Though it is just 23 miles on Shelter Cove Road, it takes an hour because it's windy and goes down to one lane at one section.

Pilots can fly into the **Shelter Cove Airport** (707/986-7447, www.sheltercove-ca.gov/airport/airport.htm) if weather conditions cooperate.

SINKYONE WILDERNESS STATE PARK

Encompassing the southern section of the Lost Coast, the **Sinkyone Wilderness State Park** (707/986-7711, www.parks.ca.gov) is a wild

Needle Rock

The easiest accessible spot in the northern Sinkyone is **Needle Rock,** the former sight of a small settlement and the current location of a park visitor center. The area's namesake rock is nearby on a black sand beach. Visitors can camp at five creekside environmental campsites (first come, first served, $5) as well as an old barn (first come, first served, $30). Camping is done by self-registration. To reach Needle Rock, head off U.S. 101 at the Garberville exit and take Redwood Road to Redway. Drive Briceland Road in Redway until it becomes Mendocino County Road 435. The road dead-ends into the state park. The last 3.5 miles are unpaved, steep, and narrow.

Needle Rock's visitors center was once a ranch house. Now it is staffed by a volunteer year-round. The visitors center has information on the region's history and various artifacts. You can also purchase maps and firewood here.

Usal Beach

Located at the southern tip of Sinkyone Wilderness State Park, **Usal Beach** is a remote, two-mile black sand beach under cliffs bristling with massive trees. It's accessible to adventurous coastal explorers via a steep, unpaved six-mile dirt road that is not for the faint-hearted or the squeamish. Passenger cars can make the drive until the winter rainy season, when four-wheel drive becomes necessary. To find it, drive about an hour north of Fort Bragg on Highway 1 and then turn left on an unmarked road at mile marker 90.88.

When you reach the beach, you can fish from shore or beachcomb the sandy expanse.

Watch sea lions torpedo through the ocean and pelicans splash into the water looking for food. Facilities include 35 primitive drive-in campsites (first come, first served, $25) with picnic tables, fire pits, and pit toilets. The rangers come here to collect the camping fees on some days, but otherwise you self register to camp. Be aware that although firearms are not allowed in the park, locals sometimes shoot guns at night here.

Eureka and Vicinity

The town of Eureka began as a seaward access point to the remote gold mines of the Trinity area. Almost immediately, settlers realized the value of the redwood trees surrounding them and started building a logging industry as well. By the late 19th century, people were getting rich and some building lovely Victorian homes as well as commercial buildings downtown. Today, lumber is still a major industry in Eureka, but because of the Victorian charm and lumber-baron history that pervade the town, tourism is another industry. Come to wander the five-block-long boardwalk on Humboldt Bay and the charming downtown shopping area or to enjoy the art sprouting up all over, including colorful murals on the sides of buildings and sculptures along the city streets. (If you drive through Eureka on U.S. 101, you'll definitely miss the best aspects of the city.) Outdoors enthusiasts can fish and hike, while history buffs can explore museums, Victorian mansions, and even a working historic mill.

SIGHTS
Blue Ox Millworks and Historic Park
Even in a town that thrives on the history of lumber, the **Blue Ox Millworks and Historic Park** (1 X St., 707/444-3437 or 800/248-4259, www.blueoxmill.com, tours Mon.-Fri. 9am-5pm, Sat. 9am-4pm, adults $7.50, over age 64 $6.50, ages 6-12 $3.50) is special. Blue Ox has a working lumber mill, an

upscale wood and cabinetry shop, a ceramics studio, a blacksmith forge, an old-fashioned print shop, a shipbuilding yard, a school, a rose garden, and a historic park. It also has the world's largest collection of human-powered woodworking tools made by the historic Barnes Equipment Company. The Blue Ox owners, Eric and Viviana Hollenbeck, didn't intend to start an immense historical enterprise; they just couldn't afford new power tools for their shop, so they rescued and rehabilitated 19th-century human-powered jigsaws, routers, and other woodworking tools. Today, the rambling buildings are filled with purchased, donated, and rehabbed tools of all kinds, which craftspeople use to create ornate custom items for homes and historic buildings across the country. The school teaches high school students about things like digging their own clay, making pottery, and hand-setting type to print their own yearbooks. Newer workshops feature a glassblowing kiln and a darkroom where students can learn "historic" (that is, nondigital) photography methods, making their own photosensitive paper and developing black-and-white and sepia prints "just the way they did at Gettysburg." Visitors to the Blue Ox learn about the real lives and times of craftspeople of the late 1800s and early 1900s as they tour the facilities and examine the equipment. If you ask, you might be allowed to touch and even work a piece of wood of your own. Also, be sure to stop in at

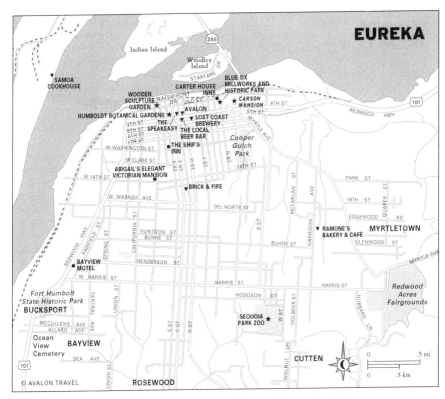

the gift shop—a converted lumberjack barracks—to check out the ceramics and woodwork the students have for sale.

Carson Mansion

Gables, turrets, cupolas, and pillars: the **Carson Mansion** (143 M St., www.ingomar.org, view only from the outside) has all these architectural flourishes. The three-story, 18-room, elaborate Victorian mansion was built by William Carson in 1884 and 1885 after he struck it rich in the lumber business. Almost demolished in the 1940s, it was purchased and renovated by local businesses that formed the Ingomar Club, which now uses it for private dinner parties. It's touted as one of the most photographed buildings in the country, but you'll have be satisfied with a picture from the street; the building and grounds are not open to the public.

Clarke Historical Museum

The privately-owned **Clarke Historical Museum** (240 E St., 707/443-1947, www.clarkemuseum.org, Wed.-Thurs. 11am-4pm, Fri.-Sat. 11am-6pm, adults $3, under age 5 free) is dedicated to preserving the history of Eureka and the surrounding area. Changing exhibitions illuminate the Native American history of the area as well as the gold rush and logging eras. The Nealis Hall annex displays one of the best collections of Native American artifacts in the state.

Fort Humboldt State Historic Park

Established in 1853 to protect white settlers—particularly gold miners—from the local Native Americans, the original Fort Humboldt lasted only 17 years as a military

EUREKA VICINITY

© AVALON TRAVEL

industry, along with examples of the type and size of redwood trees loggers were cutting and removing from 19th-century forests. Finally, you can spend a few minutes enjoying the tranquil historic garden, where master gardeners maintain the type of garden fort residents kept here 150 years ago.

Sequoia Park Zoo

The **Sequoia Park Zoo** (3414 W St., 707/441-4263, www.sequoiaparkzoo.net, summer daily 10am-5pm, winter Tues.-Sun. 10am-5pm, adults $6, seniors $5, ages 3-12 $4) might seem small, but its mission is a big one: It seeks not only to entertain visitors but also to preserve local species and educate the public about their needs. The "Secrets of the Forest" exhibit recreates the ecology of the Northern California forest while allowing visitors to see the multifarious species that live here. Be sure to say hi to Bill the Chimpanzee.

Wooden Sculpture Garden

Conveniently located downtown in the shopping district, the **Wooden Sculpture Garden of Romano Gabriel** (315 2nd St., www.eurekaheritage.org) is behind a glass wall for all to see. Romano Gabriel was a furniture maker, carpenter, and gardener who immigrated from Mura, Italy to Eureka in 1913, creating the bright colorful artworks over many years and placing them in his front yard. The Eureka Heritage Society now preserves and maintains this sculpture garden for all to enjoy.

Humboldt Botanical Gardens

Staff and local volunteers have worked for years to create **Humboldt Botanical Gardens** (College of the Redwoods, 7351 Tompkins Hill Rd., 707/442-5139, www.hbgf.org, summer Wed.-Sat. 10am-2pm and first Sun. of the month 11am-3pm, adults $5, under age 12 free), a celebration of the ecosystems of Humboldt County. The 44-acre site includes native plants, ornamental plants, and plants that grow in riparian regions.

installation. Today, **Fort Humboldt State Historic Park** (3431 Fort Ave., 707/445-6567, www.parks.ca.gov, daily 8am-5pm) gives visitors a glimpse into the lives of 19th-century soldiers and loggers. In its early days, it was home to a young Ulysses S. Grant. The original fort hospital now serves as a museum. A sedate but fairly long walking tour takes you through recreations of historic fort buildings, then out to the logging display, where you'll find several "steam donkeys," a piece of equipment that revolutionized the logging

STUART THORNTON

Eureka's most photographed building: the Carson Mansion

ENTERTAINMENT AND EVENTS

Bars

The biggest and most popular restaurant and bar in Eureka is definitely the **Lost Coast Brewery & Café** (617 4th St., 707/445-4480, www.lostcoast.com, Sun.-Thurs. 11am-10pm, Fri.-Sat. 11am-11pm). The tall cream-and-green building is perched off by itself on the main drag, easy to spot as you pass through town. The brewery draws crowds, especially on weekends, and makes popular microbrews including Great White and Downtown Brown, which are on tap here. Come for tasty brewpub-style food, and try one or more of the delicious beers.

As the name suggests, **The Local Beer Bar** (517 F St., 707/497-6320, Mon.-Thurs. 4pm-10pm, Fri.-Sat. 4pm-11pm, Sun. 2pm-8pm) is all about local beers. Chalkboard painted skateboards behind the bar announce the rotating 22 beers on tap, which always include Humboldt brews like Redwood Curtain and Mad River as well as rarities such as barrel-aged and sour beers. This great little beer hall has modern, creative touches like a bar made out of keg coolers, tabletops made from road signs, and local art decorating the walls.

Located in Opera Alley, **The Speakeasy** (411 Opera Alley, 707/444-2244, Sun.-Thurs. 4pm-11pm, Fri.-Sat. 4pm-1:30am) is the place to go in Eureka for tasty cocktails. This dark, narrow bar, which sometimes has live music, serves up Southern-style drinks, including a great mint julep.

For a solid dive-bar experience, spend an evening at **The Shanty** (213 3rd St., 707/444-2053, daily noon-2am). Hang out indoors and listen to the inspired mix of tunes from the jukebox, or the occasional live musicians. Head outdoors to play ping-pong or pool or smoke a cigarette. The extended happy hour (Mon.-Fri. 4pm-7pm, Sat.-Sun. noon-4pm) offers top-shelf beers and liquors and rock-bottom prices.

Live Music

A restored theater in downtown Eureka, the **Arkley Center for the Performing Arts** (412 G St., 707/442-1956, www.arkleycenter.com) is the home of the Eureka Symphony and North Coast Dance. The elegant venue, which has chandeliers hanging from its ceilings, also hosts rock, country, and jazz acts. Walking around downtown Eureka, you can't miss the Arkley due to the striking mural of musicians and dancers on the back of the building.

Theater

Eureka's **North Coast Repertory Theater** (300 5th St., 707/442-6278, www.ncrt.net, $15-20, cash only) performs a mix of musicals, comedies, and the occasional Shakespeare or heavy-duty drama. Many performances benefit local charities.

Events

Music lovers flock to Eureka each year for a number of big music festivals. **Blues by the Bay** (Halvorsen Park, 707/445-3378, www.bluesbythebay.org, all-weekend pass $75-95, individual events $25-55) is one of the largest. Held at Halvorsen Park on Humboldt Bay, the two-day festival in early September features many of the finest blues musicians alive playing in a spectacular setting. Accompanying the wailing blues are art, food, and microbrew booths.

Another big event is the **Redwood Coast Jazz Festival** (various venues around town, 707/445-3378, www.redwoodjazz.org, all-event pass $25-85, individual events $10-50). For four days in March, music lovers can enjoy every style of jazz imaginable, including Dixieland, zydeco, and big band. The festival also features dance contests and silent-movie screenings.

SHOPPING

The Eureka antiques scene is the largest California antiques market north of the Bay Area. In Old Town and downtown, seekers find treasures from the lumber baron-era and Victorian delights, from tiny porcelain figurines to huge pieces of furniture. **Annex 39** (610 F St., 707/443-1323, Mon.-Fri. noon-5:30pm, Sat. by appointment) specializes in vintage linens and laundry products and also has a great selection of art deco and mid-century modern pieces. **Heritage Antique & Coins** (521 4th St., 707/444-2908, Tues.-Sat. 10am-5pm) is a coin shop that also carries jewelry and Native American artifacts. Generalists will love rooting through the huge **Antiques and Goodies** (1128 3rd St,, 707/442-0445, www.antiquesandgoodies.com, Wed.-Sat. 10am-5pm and by appointment) and **Old Town Antiques** (318 F St., 707/442-3235, Mon.-Sat. 10:30am-5:30pm).

For an afternoon of shopping in Eureka, head down toward the water to 2nd Street. Most of the buildings here are historic, and you might find an unassuming brass plaque describing the famous brothel that once inhabited what is now a toy store. Literature lovers have a nice selection of independent bookstores: **Eureka Books** (426 2nd St., 707/444-9593, www.eurekabooksellers.com, daily 10am-6pm) has a big airy room in which to browse a selection of new and used books. **Booklegger** (402 2nd St., at E St., 707/445-1344, Mon.-Sat. 10am-5:30pm, Sun. 11am-4pm), just down the street, is a small but well-organized new-and-used bookshop that specializes in antique books.

Galleries and gift shops abound, highlighting various aspects of California culture. The **Sewell Gallery Fine Art** (423 F St., 707/269-0617, www.sewellgallery.com, Tues.-Sat. 10am-6pm, Sun. noon-5pm) showcases the visual artworks of 50 regional artists from painters to glass makers. **Many Hands Gallery** (438 2nd St., 877/445-0455, www.manyhandsgallery.net, Mon.-Sat. 9:30am-9pm, Sun. 10am-6pm) represents approximately 100 local artisans and also displays work from national and international artists cooperatives, fair-trade organizations, and commercial importers. The offerings are eclectic, representing many cultural, spiritual, and religious traditions from around the globe. Don't get the idea that this place is sanctimonious, though; you'll find plenty of humor and whimsy, and prices range from 10 cents to $10,000.

SPORTS AND RECREATION
Fishing

Eureka is a serious fishing destination. Oodles

of both ocean and river fishing opportunities abound all over the region, and several fishing tournaments are held each year. Anywhere in California, you must have a valid state fishing license to fish in either the ocean or the rivers. Check with your charter service or guide to be sure they provide a day license with your trip. If they don't, you will have to get your own.

For deep-sea fishing, **Celtic Charter Service** (Woodley Island Marina, Dock D, 707/442-7115, www.shellbacksportfishing.com, fishing mid-May-Sept., crabbing Nov., salmon and rockfish trips $140 pp, halibut fishing $160 pp, albacore $200 pp, crabbing $65 pp) offers excursions leaving daily at 6:30am and returning at 2pm-3pm. Prices vary, as different fishing methods allow for different numbers of people on the boat. The company rents out tackle and sells day licenses as well. **Full Throttle Sportfishing** (Woodley Island Marina, 707/498-7473, www.fullthrottlesportfishing.com, $150-250) supplies all needed tackle and can take you out to fish for salmon, rockfish, tuna, or halibut. Trips last all day, and most leave at 6:30am. If you're launching your own boat, public launches are the **Samoa Boat Ramp** (New Navy Base Rd., daily 5am-midnight) and the **Fields Landing Boat Ramp** (Railroad Ave.), both managed by Humboldt County Public Works (1106 2nd St., 707/445-7491, http://co.humboldt.ca.us, Mon.-Fri. 8am-noon and 1pm-5pm).

Eureka also has good spots for pier fishing. In town, try the K Street Pier, the pier at the east end of Commercial Street, or the pier at the end of Del Norte Street. Farther north, the north jetty (Hwy. 255, across Samoa Bridge) also has a public pier open for fishing.

Bird-Watching

The national, state, and county parks lacing the Eureka area create ideal bird-watching conditions. The **Humboldt Bay National Wildlife Refuge Complex** (1020 Ranch Rd., Loleta, 707/733-5406, www.fws.gov/humboldtbay) encompasses several wildlife-refuge sites where visitors are welcome. At the Salmon Creek Unit, you'll find the **Richard J. Guadagno**

Headquarters and Visitors Center (daily 8am-5pm), which is an excellent starting place for a number of wildlife walks. To get to the visitors center from U.S. 101, take the exit for Hookton heading north and turn left onto Eel River Drive. Take the first right onto Ranch Road, and you'll find the visitors center parking lot.

Hiking and Biking

Not only is there a vast system of trails in the state and national parks, the city of Eureka maintains a number of multiuse biking and hiking trails as well. Most familiar is the Old Town Boardwalk, part of the **Waterfront Trail** that comprises disconnected sections along Humboldt Bay. **Sequoia Park Trail** begins at the Sequoia Park Zoo and wends through redwood forests, past a duck pond, and through a meadow. This trail is paved and friendly for strollers and wheelchairs. The unpaved **Elk River Trail** (end of Hilfiker Lane) stretches for one mile through wild meadows along the coast. **Cooper Gulch Trail** is a more sedate stroll than a strenuous hike, circling the Cooper Gulch park playing fields.

Kayaking, Rafting, and Stand Up Paddleboarding

The water is cold, but getting out on it in a kayak can be exhilarating. If you're new to the sport or just want a guided trip of the area, guided paddles, lessons, rentals, and kayak fishing trips are available through **Humboats Kayak Adventures** (Woodley Island Marina, 707/443-5157, www.humboats.com, canoe and kayak rentals $25-75, 2-hour full-moon kayak tour $50). Guides lead a huge variety of tours, from serene paddles in the harbor suitable for children to 30-mile-plus trips designed for experienced kayakers.

River rafters and kayakers have great opportunities for rapids fun on the inland Klamath and Trinity Rivers. **Bigfoot Rafting Company** (Willow Creek, 530/629-2263 or 800/722-2223, www.bigfootrafting.com, adults $69-89, youth $59-79) leads half-day, full-day, and multiday trips on both rivers as well as on the

Cal-Salmon and the Smith Rivers. Experts can take inflatable kayaks down the Class IV rapids, and newcomers can find a gentle paddle with just enough white water to make things interesting.

You can also explore Humboldt Bay from the top of a stand up paddleboard. **All Out SUP** (5339 Meyers Ave., 707/616-0532, www.alloutsup.com, $75 pp) teaches beginners the basics before embarking on a tour around Woodley Island.

ACCOMMODATIONS

With such a wealth of Victorian houses, Eureka is a natural location for classic bed-and-breakfast accommodations. Chain motels are also available in abundance, many of them quite cheap. But for a real taste of the town, try one of the charming inns.

Under $150

Originally built by one of the town's founders, **Abigail's Elegant Victorian Mansion** (1406 C St., 707/444-3144, www.eureka-california.com, $89-170) offers an authentic Victorian experience. The owners have taken pains to learn the history of the house and the town and have added appropriate decor to create a truly Victorian mansion, right down to the vintage books in the elegant library. The inn also retains many of the large home's original fixtures. Anyone with an interest in Victoriana need only ask for a tour, and the owners will gladly take an hour or more to describe the artifacts in each room. Each of the five guest rooms comes with its own story and an astonishing collection of antiques. All guest rooms have private baths, although they might be across the hall. While you're not encouraged to bring small children to this romantic inn, families and groups traveling together can request combined rooms with additional beds. Abigail's recently instituted "economic stimulus pricing," which means it lowered all the room rates. In order to make that possible, they no longer serve breakfast, but it's still a lovely place to stay.

If B&Bs just aren't your style, get a room at the **Bayview Motel** (2844 Fairfield St., 707/442-1673 or 866/725-6813, www.bayviewmotel.com, $110-175). This hilltop motel has lovely views of Humboldt Bay from many of the guest rooms and from the grounds. Guest rooms are spacious and decorated in slightly more elegant colors and fabrics than at the average chain motel. You'll find wonderful whirlpool suites, free Wi-Fi, cable TV, wet bars, and coffeemakers. If you're traveling with the family, you can rent a double suite—two rooms with an adjoining door and separate baths. Although not right in downtown Eureka, it's an easy drive from the Bayview for dinner, shopping, and strolling by the harbor.

$150-250

The Ship's Inn (821 D St., 707/443-7583 or 877/443-7583, www.shipsinn.net, $140-180) is a newish B&B in an oldish, recently restored Victorian home on the east side of town. Few guest rooms and a friendly innkeeper make a stay at this inn delightfully like staying in a friend's grand home. Breakfast is particularly good, and the small garden is the perfect place to sit out in the afternoon reading a good book. Each of the three guest rooms has its own decoration and theme; the Captain's Quarters take the inn's name to heart with a blue-and-gold nautical design, while the other guest rooms tend more toward classic Victorian floral. Unlike many B&Bs, you'll find TVs in every room, along with fireplaces, plush robes, and private baths.

The **🄲 Carter House Inns** (301 L St., 800/404-1390, www.carterhouse.com, $179-495) have a range of accommodations in a cluster of butter-yellow Victorian buildings near the Carson Mansion. The main building has 23 rooms with knotty pine furniture and carpeted floors. A number of the deluxe rooms and suites in the main house have gas fireplaces and soaking tubs. Across the street, a reproduction of a Victorian mansion has six rooms, including a family suite with two bedrooms, while **The Bell Cottage** has three rooms and a full common kitchen. If you really want to splurge, rent **The Carter Cottage,** which has two bathrooms, a back deck with a fountain, a soaking tub, and a large den and kitchen area. No matter where you choose to stay, you'll be treated to a hot breakfast and an afternoon wine and appetizer hour. You can also dine or snack in the inn's renowned Restaurant 301. Warning: You may never want to leave.

FOOD
American
The 🄲 **Samoa Cookhouse** (511 Vance Rd., Samoa, 707/442-1659, www.samoacookhouse.net, summer daily 7am-9pm, winter daily 7am-8pm, $16) is a historic Eureka institution. Red-checked tablecloths cover long, rough tables to recreate the atmosphere of a logging-camp dining hall. The all-you-can-eat meals are served family-style from huge serving platters. Diners sit on benches and pass the hearty fare down in turn. Think big hunks of roast beef, mountains of mashed potatoes, and piles of cooked vegetables. This is the place to bring your biggest appetite. After dinner, browse the small Historic Logging Museum and gift shop.

Restaurant 301 (301 L St., 800/404-1390, www.carterhouse.com, daily 6pm-9pm, $24-35) at the Carter House Inns seems like a top-shelf San Francisco or Los Angeles eatery lost on the distant North Coast. The chef creates an ever-changing menu of delectable delicacies, with tasting menus that give diners the best chance to experience this great restaurant. On the succession of plates served at a relaxed pace, you'll find everything from exotic duck dishes to simple local seafood preparations to items from the restaurant's own on-site kitchen garden. For a special treat, try the wine flights suggested with the menus. Restaurant 301 is known for their extensive wine list with over 3,400 selections.

Another high-end Eureka restaurant that impresses even the most discriminating Bay Area-trained palates is **Avalon** (239 G St., 707/445-0500, www.avaloneureka.com, Tues.-Sun. 5pm-9pm, $20-28), a restaurant that speaks to the hearts of eco-conscious carnivores with sustainably sourced steaks, mixed grills, and game meats prominent on the menu.

The **Surfside Burger Shack** (445 5th St., 707/268-1295, Mon.-Sat. 11am-9pm, Sun. 11am-8pm, $5.50-8) is nowhere near the ocean. It's actually right on a busy Eureka street. But the shack does have surfing decor and darn good burgers made from grass-fed Humboldt cows. The classic cheeseburger hits the spot, but the shack also gets creative with the beef. For example, the "Surfside Sunrise" is a burger topped with cheese, bacon, an egg, and maple syrup.

Bakeries
Ramone's Bakery & Café (209 E St., 707/445-2923, Mon.-Fri. 7am-6pm, Sat. 8am-5pm, Sun. 8am-4pm; 2297 Harrison Ave., 707/442-1336, Mon.-Sat. 6:30am-9pm, Sun. 7:30am-7pm) is a genuine local North Coast chain. All locations (including one in Arcata and one in McKinleyville) sell fresh from-scratch baked goods and candies. Come in the morning to enjoy a fresh cup of coffee roasted in-house and a Danish or a scone, indulge in an afternoon pastry, or even get a whole tart, cake, or loaf of fresh-baked bread to take out for an afternoon picnic.

Italian
Brick & Fire Bistro (1630 F St., 707/268-8959, www.brickandfirebistro.com, Mon. and Wed.-Thurs. 11:30am-8:30pm, Fri. 11:30am-9pm, Sat. 5pm-9pm, Sun. 5pm-8:30pm, $14-22) updates Italian classics with a menu that includes fire-roasted polenta lasagna and pizzas with ingredients like locally smoked salmon and quail eggs.

INFORMATION AND SERVICES
The **Humboldt County Convention and Visitors Bureau** does not operate a public visitors center, but if you need something, drop by the business office (1034 2nd St., 800/346-3482, www.redwoods.info, Mon.-Fri. 9am-5pm) and they'll do their best to help you. The website is an ideal place to do research

on vacation plans anywhere in the Redwood Coast region, and you can call the travel hotline (800/346-3482) for information.

The **Eureka Chamber of Commerce** (2112 Broadway, 707/442-3738, www.eurekachamber.com, Mon.-Fri. 8:30am-5pm) runs a helpful facility, with plenty of literature about things to do in town and beyond.

The *Times-Standard* (www.times-standard.com) covers both national and local news and includes information about events in the North Coast region. You can pick up a copy at many businesses around the region. Check the entertainment section for the latest hot spots and live events during your stay.

As the big urban area on the North Coast, Eureka and Arcata have the major services travelers may need. You'll find branches of major banks, complete with ATMs, which are also available at supermarkets, pharmacies, and other businesses.

Naturally, you'll find **post offices** (337 W. Clark St., 707/442-1768, Mon.-Fri. 8:30am-5pm, Sat. noon-3pm; 514 H St., 707/442-0856, Mon.-Fri. 8:30am-5pm).

Eureka has a full-service hospital, **St. Joseph Hospital** (2700 Dolbeer St., 707/445-8121, www.stjosepheureka.org), with an emergency room and an urgent care center for less serious issues.

GETTING THERE AND AROUND

Eureka is on U.S. 101, easily accessed by car from north or south. From Crescent City, Eureka is less than an hour's drive south on U.S. 101.

In Eureka, driving is the only option if you're not staying downtown, especially if you want to head out to Woodley Island. You can easily visit the 2nd Street shops and restaurants on foot. Parking downtown is metered or free on the streets, and not too difficult to find except on holiday or event weekends.

Bus service in and around Eureka is operated by the **Humboldt Transit Authority** (HTA, www.hta.org, adults $1.40, children and seniors $1.10). The HTA's **Eureka Transit System** (ETS) runs within town limits, and the **Redwood Transit System** (RTS, www.redwoodtransit.org, adults $2.75, children and seniors $2.50) can take you around the area, from Eureka north to Crescent City, south to Ferndale, and east to Willow Creek.

Eureka has a small commercial airport, **Arcata-Eureka Airport** (ACV, 3561 Boeing Ave., McKinleyville, 707/839-5401, http://co.humboldt.ca.us/aviation), that serves the North Coast region. You can fly in and out on Horizon Air (a division of Alaska) or United Airlines. Expect flights to be expensive but convenient.

Arcata

Located on the northern shore of barbell-shaped Humboldt Bay, Arcata has a distinctly different feel than its southern neighbor. The hippie daughter of blue-collar Eureka, Arcata is home to Humboldt State University. Students make up almost half of the city's population, and the town has become known for its liberal politics; at one point the city council was made up mostly of Green Party members. This progressive atmosphere feels a world away from most of the other small towns in the region.

With about half the population of Eureka, Arcata has a small town atmosphere. The heart of Arcata is the Arcata Plaza, a town park with a William McKinley statue, a couple of palm trees, and a grassy lawn. Here you'll almost always find folks hanging out, playing music, and smoking non-tobacco cigarettes. Circling the plaza are independent restaurants, bars, coffee shops, and stores selling items like shirts made out of hemp. (A local law limits chains and franchises downtown.)

Arcata has a lively arts and music scene along with a handful of restaurants that you might expect in a bigger city. It makes a great home base for exploring the wild North Coast.

SIGHTS
🄲 Arcata Community Forest

The first city-owned forest in California, the 2,134-acre **Arcata Community Forest** (east ends of 11th St., 14th St., and California St., 707/822-5951, www.cityofarcata.org) has trails winding through second-growth redwoods, open for hiking, mountain biking, and horseback riding. Just east of the city's downtown and behind Humboldt State University, the forest is an ideal place to stroll between the silent giants, many of which are cloaked in moss, and take in stumps the size of compact cars and vibrant green waist-high ferns. The park also has a section with picnic tables and a playground.

Arcata Marsh and Wildlife Sanctuary

Believe it or not, one of Arcata's most popular places to take a hike is in a section of their wastewater treatment facility. The **Arcata Marsh Interpretive Center** (569 S. G St., 707/826-2359, www.cityofarcata.org, Tues.-Sun. 9am-5pm, Mon. 1pm-5pm) is an information station with a small museum that explains how the city transformed an industrial wasteland into a 307-acre wildlife sanctuary using Arcata's wastewater. You can also hike the sanctuary's five miles of hiking and biking paths, or try to spot some of the 270 bird species that now use the marsh as a migratory stop.

ENTERTAINMENT AND EVENTS
Bars

A strip of dive bars lines the edge of Arcata Plaza on 9th Street. The best of the bunch, **The Alibi** (744 9th St., 707/822-3731, www.thealibi.com, daily 8am-2am), dates back to the 1920s. The Alibi serves cheap, well-crafted cocktails, including a wide range of Bloody Marys. It also has an extensive breakfast, lunch, and dinner menu with 28 specialty burgers and entrées from burger steaks to organic tofu cutlets.

A few feet away, **Everett's Club** (784 9th St., 707/822-2291, Tues. 3pm-5pm and 9pm-1am,

Wed.-Thurs. 6pm-2am, Fri. 2pm-2am, Sat. 8am-2am, Sun. 4pm-5pm and 9pm-1am) is a place where you can drink with the locals while big game heads mounted on the walls stare down at you. Out back is a small patio for the smoking crowd.

Humboldt Brews (856 10th St., 707/826-2739, www.humboldtbrews.com, daily noon-11pm except music nights when it stays open until 2am) serves 25 beers on tap, as well as food. This popular hangout also has a pool table and an adjacent room that serves as a concert space.

Live Music

Music legends play at Humboldt State University's **John Van Duzer Theatre** (1 Harpst St., 707/826-4411, www.humboldt.edu, check website for schedule). Elvis Costello, Ziggy Marley, and Alison Krauss have all graced its stage. Up and coming acts visit campus as well, typically performing at **The Depot** (University Center, 1 Harpst St., 707/826-4411).

Humboldt Brews (856 10th St., 707/826-2739, www.humboldtbrews.com, daily noon-11pm except music nights when it stays open until 2am) hosts mid-sized national jam bands, indie acts, and reggae outfits.

Funk bands fill up the dance floor at **Jambalaya** (915 H St., 707/822-4766, www.jambalayaarcata.com, Mon.-Fri. 9am-2am, Sat.-Sun. 10pm-2am), a few feet away from Arcata Plaza. The kitchen serves up New Orleans-style po'boys.

Festivals and Events

Arcata Plaza is the starting line of the **Kinetic Grand Championship** (Memorial Day weekend, http://kineticgrandchampionship.com), a three-day, 42-mile race featuring human-powered art sculptures that continues on to Eureka and Ferndale.

Also in the plaza is June's annual **Arcata Main Street Oyster Festival** (www.oysterfestival.net), which celebrates the local Kumamoto oyster with—you guessed it—oysters. There's also live music and flowing micro-brewed beer.

Cinema

Dating back to 1938, the art deco **Arcata Theatre Lounge** (1036 G St., 707/822-1220, www.arcatatheatre.com) screens movies, hosts concerts, and hosts events like "Sci-Fi Pint and Pizza Night," where they show old science fiction movies. The theater seats have been replaced by circular tables and chairs, and the full bar serves food as well as drinks, making it a perfect place for a night out.

A few blocks away, the 1914 **Minor Theatre** (1001 H St., 707/822-3456, www.catheatres. com) is one of the oldest still operating movie theaters in the country, showing independent movies as well as Hollywood films.

SPORTS AND RECREATION

Both the **Arcata Community Forest** (east ends of 11th St., 14th St. and California St., 707/822-5951, www.cityofarcata.org) and the **Arcata Marsh and Wildlife Sanctuary** (569 S. G St., 707/826-2359, www.cityofarcata. org) have miles of hiking trails. The **Redwood Canopy Tour** (786/200-4260, www.north-coastadventurecenters.com, $75 for 2-3 hours) offers a more adventurous approach to the Community Forest: ascending 70-100 feet into the redwood canopy and then using a zip line to travel among the treetops.

The famous 18-hole **Redwood Curtain Disc Golf Course** (accessible from Humboldt State University's Redwood Science Lab, though parking is only available in the lot after 5pm, www.parinfinity.org) winds its way through massive redwood trees. On the second hole, the tee is located atop a 10-foot high redwood stump. Sunday mornings at 11:11am, random double matches take place.

For local sports action, get a ticket to see the **Humboldt Crabs** (Arcata Ball Park, F St. and 9th St., 707/826-2333, http://humboldtcrabs. com), the oldest continually-operated collegiate summer baseball team in the country.

SHOPPING

There are shops located around Arcata Plaza and along H Street, which has a number of unique stores. Head into **Pacific Paradise** (1087 H St., 707/822-7143, Mon.-Sat. 10am-7pm, Sun. 10:30am-6:30pm) to stock up on Humboldt County essentials like golf discs, hoodies, tie-dyes, and smoking equipment.

Across the street, the **Tin Can Mailman Used & Rare Books Store** (1000 H St., 707/822-1307, www.tincanbooks.com, Mon.-Sat. 10am-7pm, Sun. 11am-6pm) crams together two full floors full of used books. If you'd rather get the latest fiction or memoir, head over to **Northtown Books** (957 H St., 707/822-2834, www.northtownbooks.com, Mon.-Thurs. and Sat. 10am-7pm, Fri. 10am-9pm, Sun. noon-5pm). They also have an extensive magazine collection.

Solutions (858 G St., 707/822-6972) is right on the plaza and the place to pick up hemp clothing, organic bedding, and eco-goods.

A few blocks from the plaza, **Holly Yashi** (1300 9th St., 707/822-5132, www.hol-lyyashi.com, Mon.-Sat. 10am-6pm) specializes in niobium jewelry. Niobium is a metal that gains streaks of color after being dipped in an electrically charged bath. You can watch artists at work crafting the jewelry in the attached studio.

ACCOMMODATIONS

Downtown lodging options are surprisingly limited. The **Hotel Arcata** (708 9th St., 707/826-0217, www.hotelarcata.com, $88-159) is nothing fancy, but it has a superb location right on the plaza. The rooms are small, but all the bathrooms have claw foot tubs outfitted with showerheads. The bottom floor of the hotel is home to the popular Tomo Japanese Restaurant as well as a gift shop and beauty salon.

The **Lady Anne Bed and Breakfast** (902 14th St., 707/822-2797, http://ladyanneinn. com, $115-220) has a little more character, with five rooms in an old Victorian from 1888. All have private bathrooms and most include gas-burning woodstoves. A music room is decorated with all sorts of instruments including a piano, an accordion, and a bass guitar that guests are allowed to play. Like all good B&Bs, the Lady Anne serves a full, hot breakfast.

© STUART THORNTON

Arcata Plaza

A few miles from the Plaza, the **Best Western Arcata Inn** (4827 Valley West Blvd., 707/826-0313, http://bestwesterncalifornia.com, $109) is a well-regarded chain motel option in the area. The rooms have satellite TV and Wi-Fi, and there's a swimming pool and hot tub on the grounds.

FOOD

For a small city, Arcata has a lot of worthwhile dining options. Many of the restaurants are committed to using ingredients from local Humboldt farms and ranches.

American

Almost everything served up or sat on in **Luke's Joint** (887 H St., 707/826-0415, www.lukesjointarcata.com, daily 9am-8pm, $7-13) is made in Humboldt County. The produce hails from local farms and the furniture is made by local companies. Luckily, this small eatery has more to recommend it than its dedication to the local economy. Luke's serves big, tasty hot sandwiches, wraps, and salads for breakfast, lunch, and dinner. Be sure to review the section of the menu titled "Sublime Swine," which has a series of smoked pork shoulder sandwiches and tacos.

French

Renata's Creperie and Espresso (1030 G St., 707/825-8783, Tues.-Thurs. and Sun. 8am-3pm, Fri.-Sat. 8am-3pm and 5pm-9pm, $4-12) is the best place to start the day. Their organic buckwheat crepes are artfully decorated with drizzled sauces and well-placed garnishes, and deliver on their promising looks with sweet and savory fillings. Renata's is also open for dinner on Friday and Saturday nights.

Italian

Named for a region in Central Italy, **Abruzzi** (780 7th St., 707/826-2345, www.abruzziarcata.com, daily 5pm-9pm, $12-40) is the place to go for fine dining around the plaza. The menu includes free-range chicken dishes, seafood offerings, and classic pastas like Bolognese, primavera, and alfredo.

Japanese

A local institution for almost 30 years, **Tomo Japanese Restaurant** (708 9th St., 707/822-1414, www.tomoarcata.com, Mon.-Sat. 11:30am-2pm and 5pm-9pm, Sun. 5pm-9pm, $10-22) serves sushi rolls and other entrées that are as eclectic as its hometown. Get a spicy tofu roll or a truly unique locally smoked albacore roll. Like any great sushi bar, Tomo has a list of sakes, but there's also a full bar.

Markets

Stop in **Wildberries Marketplace** (747 13th St., 707/822-0095, www.wildberries.com, daily 6am-midnight) to stock up for a picnic in the redwoods. Alongside the aisles of health foods, there's a café, juice bar, and coffee shop. Wildberries also hosts its own farmer's market (www.humfarm.org, Tues. 3:30pm-6:30pm).

The Arcata Plaza also hosts a Saturday **farmer's market** (www.humfarm.org, mid-Apr.-mid-Nov. Sat. 9am-2pm) that includes live music.

INFORMATION AND SERVICES

The **California Welcome Center** (1635 Heindon Rd., 707/822-3619, www.arcatachamber.com, daily 11am-5pm) has information on Arcata as well as the rest of California. There's also Internet access if you need to go online.

Though based in Eureka, the daily *Times-Standard* (www.times-standard.com) also covers Arcata. *The Lumberjack* (http://thelumberjack.org) is the Humboldt State University student newspaper.

Arcata has a **post office** (799 H St., 707/822-3370, www.usps.com) located right off the plaza.

The **Mad River Community Hospital** (3800 Janes Rd., 707/822-3621, http://madriverhospital.com) has an emergency room and urgent care department.

GETTING THERE AND AROUND

Arcata is eight miles north of Eureka on U.S. 101. Once there, it's easiest to just park your car and walk around the small city.

If you grow weary of walking, the **Arcata & Mad River Transit System** (www.arcatatransit.org, adults $1.50, children and seniors $1) runs a fleet of red and yellow buses that travel all over Arcata.

Nearby McKinleyville has a small commercial airport, **Arcata-Eureka Airport** (ACV, 3561 Boeing Ave., McKinleyville, 707/839-5401, http://co.humboldt.ca.us/aviation), that serves the North Coast region. You can fly in and out on United Airlines. Expect flights to be expensive but convenient.

Trinidad and Vicinity

With a population of just 360 people, Trinidad is one of the smallest incorporated cities in California; it's also one of the most beautiful. Perched on a bluff over boat-studded Trinidad Bay, Trinidad has a wealth of natural assets, including scenic headlands and wild beaches on either side of town. It also has a long history: The town was named by two Spanish Navy men who came to the area on Trinity Sunday in 1775. Located right off U.S. 101, Trinidad is worth a visit, whether it's for a stop to stretch your legs or a tranquil weekend getaway.

SIGHTS
Trinidad Memorial Lighthouse

Not an actual lighthouse but a replica of the one on nearby Trinidad Head, **Trinidad Memorial Lighthouse** (Trinity St. and Edwards St.) is the local photo opportunity. It was built by the Trinidad Civic Club in 1949 with prize money from the "Build a Better Community Contest." The small red and white building sits on a bluff above the bay where boats bob in the water. A marble slab and a series of plaques list those individuals who have been lost at sea. To the left of the lighthouse is the old Trinidad fog bell.

Trinidad Head

A rocky promontory north of the bay, the 380-foot-high **Trinidad Head** (end of Edwards St.) affords great views of the area's beaches, bay, and town. A one-mile-long loop trail on the headlands goes under canopies of vegetation and then out to a series of clear spots with benches. A large stone cross on the west end of Trinidad Head marks where Spanish seamen initially erected a wooden cross. Below the cross is a small wooden deck where you can glimpse the top of the Trinidad Head Lighthouse. The squat lighthouse on a 175-foot-high cliff was activated in 1871. In 1914, the lighthouse made news when, according to the lighthouse keeper, a huge wave extinguished the light.

Trinidad State Beach

Below the bluffs of Trinidad Head, **Trinidad State Beach** (end of Edwards St.,

© STUART THORNTON

Trinidad Memorial Lighthouse

707/677-3570, www.parks.ca.gov, daily sunrise-sunset, free) runs north for a half-mile. Spruce-tufted Pewetole Island and a scattering of scenic coastal islets lie offshore. It's a great place for a contemplative walk.

Humboldt State University Marine Laboratory

Students come to the **HSU Marine Laboratory** (570 Ewing St., 707/826-3671, www.humboldt.edu, tours by appointment only, self-guided tours $1 pp, guided tours $2 pp) to learn about the area's coastal critters. A tour of the lab includes looks at invertebrates from nearby intertidal zones.

SPORTS AND RECREATION
Kayaking and Whale-Watching

Protected Trinidad Bay is an ideal spot for a scenic sea kayaking excursion. **Humboats Kayak Adventures** (707/443-5157, www.humboats.com, $75/three-hour tour) runs guided whale-watching tours in the spring and early summer when gray whales migrate right through the protected harbor area. In the summer and fall, Humboats offers a kayak-based tour of Trinidad's headlands.

Sportfishing

If you'd rather have the satisfaction of catching your own fresh seafood, head out to sea with one of two Trinidad-based fishing outfits. Fish for rockfish, salmon, or Dungeness crab with **Trinidad Bay Charters** (707/499-8878, www.trinidadbaycharters.net) or **Patrick's Point Charters** (707/445-4106, www.patrickspointcharters.com, $100/half-day).

Surfing

South of Trinidad are some of Humboldt County's best known surf spots. **Moonstone Beach** (three miles south of Trinidad on Scenic Dr.) is a popular surf break where the Little River pours into Trinidad Bay. Up the road a half a mile, **Camel Rock** (about 2.3 miles south of Trinidad on Scenic Dr.) has right breaks that peel inside of a distinct, double-humped offshore rock.

ACCOMMODATIONS

The only lodging in Trinidad proper is the **Trinidad Bay Bed and Breakfast** (560 Edward St., 707/677-0840, www.trinidadbaybnb.com, $230-350), right across the street from the Trinidad Memorial Lighthouse. Each of the four rooms has a view of Trinidad Bay; two rooms have private entrances, and all have private bathrooms. A hot three-course breakfast is served every morning.

Between the main section of Trinidad and Patrick's Point State Park, **The Lost Whale Bed & Breakfast Inn** (3452 Patrick's Point Dr., 707/677-3425, http://lostwhaleinn.com, $270-315) has five rooms with great views of the Pacific and four with garden views. Two rooms have lofts to accommodate up to four people. There's a private trail to the beach below, an ocean-view hot tub, and a wood-burning sauna. A seven-course breakfast buffet is served every morning.

For those who want to rough it a bit, **The Emerald Forest** (753 Patrick's Point Dr., 707/677-3554, www.cabinsintheredwoods. com, $149-289) has a variety of rustic cabins for rent. The higher-end cabins have full kitchens and amenities like wood-burning stoves. RV and tent campsites are also available ($33-45), although the ones at nearby Patrick's Point State Park are more spacious.

FOOD

Stock up on delicious, locally smoked seafood at **◖ Katy's Smokehouse** (740 Edwards St., 707/677-0151, www.katyssmokehouse.com, daily 9am-6pm). There are smoked oysters and salmon jerky, but you can't go wrong with the smoked king salmon. It's not a sit-down restaurant, so you'll need to get your order to go. It's great to bring on a camping trip to the nearby parks—just don't leave it out, or you'll end up feeding it to the bears.

The friendly, spunky staff at the **Beachcomber Café** (363 Trinity St., 707/677-0106, http://trinidadbeachcomber.blogspot. com, Mon.-Fri. 7am-4pm, Sat.-Sun. 8am-4pm) serve up coffee, cookies, paninis, and bagels. It also has free Wi-Fi with a purchase.

The original café that was opened in the current spot of the **Seascape Restaurant** (1 Bay St., 707/677-3762, daily 7am-8pm, $9-17) was blown away by a massive storm in 1959. While the Seascape might not blow you away, it has a great location on Trinidad Bay. It serves seafood sandwiches, burgers, and fish and chips, and something called a "Grilled Smokey" that's little more than salmon cream cheese spread between two toasted pieces of sourdough bread. Also of interest is a breakfast entrée of scrambled eggs topped with clam chowder.

Just north of Trinidad, the **Larrupin Café** (1658 Patrick's Point Dr., 707/677-0230, www. larrupin.com, Fri.-Wed. 5pm-9pm, $20-30) mesquite barbecues everything from tofu kebabs to creole prawns. They are also known for their mustard dill and red sauces, which you can purchase to take home.

INFORMATION AND SERVICES

To plan a trip to Trinidad, visit the **Official Trinidad Visitor Chamber of Commerce** website (www.trinidadcalif.com), which has lots of great information about the small community.

Trinidad is a small city, so don't expect too many services. However, there is a **post office** (357 Main St., 707/677-3117, www.usps.com). Most major services can be found in nearby Arcata.

GETTING THERE AND AROUND

Trinidad is 15 miles north of Arcata on U.S. 101. Take the 728 exit off the highway.

The **Redwood Transit System** (707/443-0826, www.redwoodtransit.org, adults $2.75, children and seniors $2.50) has buses that connect from Arcata and Eureka to Trinidad.

◖ PATRICK'S POINT STATE PARK

Patrick's Point State Park (4150 Patrick's Point Dr., 707/677-3570, www.parks.ca.gov, day use $8) is a rambling coastal park 25 miles north of Eureka, replete with beaches, historic landmarks, trails, and campgrounds. It's not the biggest of the many parks along the North Coast, but it is one of the best. The climate remains cool year-round, making it perfect for hiking and exploring, if not for ocean swimming. There's a native plant garden, a visitors center, and three campgrounds ($35), plus a recreated Yurok Village. Because Patrick's Point is small in comparison to the other parks, it's easy to get around. Request a map at the gate and follow the signs along the tiny and often nameless park roads.

Sights

Prominent among the local landmarks is the place the park was named after: **Patrick's Point,** which offers panoramic Pacific views and can be reached by a brief hike from a convenient parking lot. Adjacent to Patrick's Point in a picturesque cove is **Wedding Rock,** a promontory sticking out into the ocean like an upturned thumb. People really do hike the narrow trail out to the rock to get married; you might even see a bride and groom stumbling along holding hands on their way back from the ceremony.

The most fascinating area in the park is **Sumeg Village,** a recreation of a native Yurok village based on an actual archaeological find east of here. Visitors can crawl through the perfectly round hobbit-like hole-doors into semi-subterranean homes, meeting places, and storage buildings. Or check out the native plant garden, a collection of local plants the Yurok people used for food, basketry, and medicine. Today, the local Yurok people use Sumeg Village as a gathering place for education and celebrations, and they request that visitors tread lightly and do not disturb this tranquil area.

Those who want to dip a toe in the ocean rather than just gaze at it from afar will be glad to know that Patrick's Point has a number of accessible beaches. The steep trail leading down to **Agate Beach** deters few visitors. This wide stretch of coarse sand bordered by cliffs shot through with shining quartz veins is perfect for lounging, playing, and beachcombing. The

© STUART THORNTON

Sumeg Village in Patrick's Point State Park

semiprecious stones for which it is named really do appear here. The best time to find good agates is in the winter, after a storm.

Hiking

Only six miles of trails thread their way through Patrick's Point. Choose from the **Rim Trail** (four miles round-trip), which will take you along the cliffs for a view of the sea and if you're lucky a view of migrating whales. Tree-lovers might prefer the **Octopus Tree Trail,** which provides a great view of an old-growth Sitka spruce grove.

Camping

The three campgrounds at Patrick's Point (information 707/677-3570, reservations 800/444-7275, www.reserveamerica.com, $35) have a total of 124 sites. It can be difficult to determine the difference between **Agate Beach, Abalone,** and **Penn Creek,** so be sure to get good directions from the park rangers when you arrive. Most campsites are pleasantly shaded by the groves of trees; all include a picnic table, fire pit, and food storage cupboard, and you'll find running water, restrooms, and showers nearby.

Information and Services

You can get a map and information at the **Patrick's Point State Park Visitors Center** (707/677-1945, summer daily 9am-5pm, winter usually daily 10am-4pm), immediately to the right when you get to the entry gate. Information about nature walks and campfire programs is posted on the bulletin board.

Getting There and Around

Patrick's Point State Park is located on the coast, 25 miles north of Eureka and 15 miles south of Orick on U.S. 101.

Redwood National and State Parks

The lands of Redwood National and State Parks (www.nps.gov/redw, day use and camping free) meander along the coast and include three state parks—Prairie Creek Redwoods, Del Norte Coast Redwoods, and Jedediah Smith. This complex of parkland encompasses most of California's northern redwood forests. The main landmass of Redwood National Park is just south of Prairie Creek State Park along U.S. 101, stretching east from the coast and the highway. To get to the park from the south, drive along Bald Hills Road.

REDWOOD NATIONAL PARK
Thomas H. Kuchel Visitors Center

If you're new to the Redwood National and State Parks, the **Thomas H. Kuchel Visitors Center** (U.S. 101, west of Orick, 707/465-7765, spring-fall daily 9am-5pm, winter daily 9am-4pm) is a large facility with a ranger station, clean restrooms, and a path to the shore. You can get maps, advice, permits for backcountry camping, and books. In the summer, rangers run patio talks and coast walks that provide a great introduction to the area for children and adults. You can also have a picnic at one of the tables outside the visitors center, or you can walk a short distance to Redwood Creek.

Trees of Mystery

Generations of kids have enjoyed spotting the gigantic wooden sculptures of Paul Bunyan and his blue ox, Babe, from U.S. 101. The **Trees of Mystery** (15500 U.S. 101 N., 707/482-2251 or 800/638-3389, www.treesofmystery.net, June-Aug. daily 8:30am-6:30pm, Sept.-May daily 9:30am-4:30pm, adults $15, seniors $11, ages 7-12 $8) doesn't disappoint as a great place to take a break from the road to let the family out for some good cheesy fun. Visitors can enjoy the original Mystery Hike, the SkyTrail gondola ride through the old-growth redwoods, and the palatial gift shop. Perhaps best of all, at the left

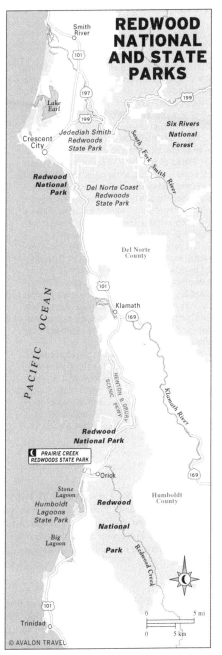

REDWOOD NATIONAL AND STATE PARKS

Smith River

101

197

199

Lake Earl

199

Jedediah Smith Redwoods State Park

Crescent City

Six Rivers National Forest

South Fork Smith River

Redwood National Park

Del Norte Coast Redwoods State Park

Del Norte County

PACIFIC OCEAN

101

Klamath

169

NEWTON B. DRURY SCENIC PKWY

Klamath River

Redwood National Park

PRAIRIE CREEK REDWOODS STATE PARK

Orick

Stone Lagoon

Humboldt County

Humboldt Lagoons State Park

Redwood

National

Big Lagoon

Park

Redwood Creek

101

Trinidad

0   5 mi

0   5 km

© AVALON TRAVEL

end of the gift shop is a little-known gem: the Native American museum. A large collection of artifacts from ethnic groups across the country and indigenous to the redwood forests grace several crowded galleries. The restrooms here are large and well-maintained, which makes Trees of Mystery a nice stop en route.

Hiking

One of the easiest, most popular ways to get close to the trees is to walk the **Lady Bird Johnson Trail** (Bald Hills Rd., 1.4 miles, easy). This nearly level loop provides an intimate view of the redwood and fir forests that define this region. It's not far from the **Thomas H. Kuchel Visitors Center** (U.S. 101, west of Orick, 707/465-7765, summer daily 9am-5pm, winter daily 9am-4pm), and the staff there can direct you to the trailhead and provide a simple map. Another easy-access trail is **Trillium Falls** (Davison Rd. at Elk Meadow, 2.8 miles, easy). You may not see elk or trillium flowers, but the redwood trees along this cool, dark trail are striking, and the small waterfall is a nice treasure in the woods. This little hike is lovely any time of year but best in spring, when the water volume over the falls is at its peak.

The **Lost Man Creek Trail** (east of Elk Meadow, 1 mile off U.S. 101, 0.5-22 miles, easy-difficult) has it all. The first 0.5 miles is perfect for wheelchair users and families with small children. But as the trail rolls along, the grades get steeper and more challenging. You can customize the length of this out-and-back trail by turning around at any time. If you reach the Lost Man Creek picnic grounds, your total round-trip distance is 22 miles with more than 3,000 feet of elevation gain and several stream crossings.

Another fabulous long hike is the **Redwood Creek Trail** (Bald Hills Rd. spur off U.S. 101, difficult), which follows Redwood Creek for eight miles to the **Tall Trees Grove.** If you have someone willing to act as a shuttle driver, you can pick up the **Tall Trees Trail** and walk another 6 miles (a total of 14 miles) to the **Dolason Prairie Trail,** which takes you back out to Bald Hills Road.

TOURIST TRAPS

the Trees of Mystery's Paul Bunyan statue

As you wend your way up U.S. 101 through the verdant forests filled with rare trees, you'll become aware of something besides parks and trails luring visitors to pull over and rest awhile. You'll know them by the collections of chainsaw carvings, the kitschy hand-painted signs, and the cheap, shiny toys out front. Whether you've found a Redwood Sculpture Emporium, a Drive-Thru Tree, or a Mystery Spot, hang on to your wallet when you stop at one of the Redwood Coast's tourist traps.

The granddaddy of all tourist traps – it's even an example of the concept in Wikipedia – is the **Trees of Mystery.** Trees of Mystery has it all: wood sculptures, a "mystery" visual-trickery trail, and a gondola ride. But most of all, it's got a gift shop the size of a supermarket selling souvenirs beyond your imagination (unless you've imagined varnished redwood slices painted with images of Jesus and the Virgin Mary).

The various Drive-Thru Trees are usually privately-owned tourist traps, and you'll pay $10-20 to drive on a tiny one-way street through a large mutilated tree. The novelty of finding trees big enough to create drive-thru tunnels catches the attention of many out-of-state visitors. And families on long road trips often shell out for the drive-thru trees to sidetrack their kids for just five more minutes.

Finally, you can't miss the roadside redwood sculpture stands. They dot the sides of the highway, selling wooden animals lovingly sculpted by chainsaw artists. You'll also find T-shirts, coffee mugs, shot glasses, and dozens of other souvenirs. Little animal figurines made out of petrified moose and elk turds are a particular favorite with the children.

Accommodations and Camping

If you want to sleep indoors but still stay close to the national park, your best bet is the **Green Valley Motel** (120784 U.S. 101, Orick, 707/488-2341, $44) in nearby Orick.

There are no designated campgrounds in Redwood National Park, but free backcountry camping is allowed; permits may be necessary in certain areas. The **Elam Camp** and the **44 Camp** are both hike-in primitive campgrounds along the Dolason Prairie Trail.

Contact the **Crescent City Information Center** (1111 2nd St., Crescent City, 707/465-7335, spring-fall daily 9am-5pm, winter daily 9am-4pm) if you're planning a backcountry camping trip. The center can help you determine whether you need a permit and issue one if you do.

Getting There and Around

The Redwood National and State Parks line U.S. 101 from Prairie Creek Redwoods in the south all the way up to Jedediah Smith near Crescent City at the northern end. The

lush Fern Canyon, in Prairie Creek Redwoods State Park

Thomas H. Kuchel Visitors Center at the south end of the park is located 40 miles north of Eureka on U.S. 101.

█ PRAIRIE CREEK REDWOODS STATE PARK

In addition to the silent majesty of the redwoods, **Prairie Creek Redwoods State Park** (Newton B. Drury Dr., 25 miles south of Crescent City, 707/465-7347, campground 707/488-2171, www.parks.ca.gov, day use $8) has miles of wild beach, roaming wildlife, and a popular hike through a one-of-a-kind fern draped canyon. The 14,000 acres of Prairie Creek offer a sampler platter of the best natural elements of the North Coast.

For wildlife enthusiasts, one of the many reasons to visit Prairie Creek is a chance to view a herd of **Roosevelt elk.** This subspecies of elk can stand up to five feet high and can weigh close to 1,000 pounds. These big guys usually hang out at—where else?—the Elk Prairie, a stretch of open grassland along the highway. The best times to see the elk are early morning and around sunset. August to October is the elk mating season, when the calls of the bulls fill the air. The elk do roam all over the park, but there's a good chance you might see some in the prairie located off the southern end of the Newton B. Drury Drive. The park asks that you stay in the viewing area and let the elk enjoy grazing in peace.

Prairie Creek Visitors Center

Just beyond the entrance off U.S. 101, the **Prairie Creek Visitors Center** (Newton B. Drury Dr., 707/488-2039, usually daily 9am-5pm) includes a small interpretive museum describing the history of the California redwood forests. A tiny bookshop adjoins the museum, well stocked with books describing the history, nature, and culture of the area. Many ranger-led programs originate at the visitors center, and permits are available for backcountry camping in the park.

Newton B. Drury Scenic Drive

A gorgeous scenic road through the redwoods,

Newton B. Drury Scenic Drive, off U.S. 101 about five miles south of Klamath, features old-growth trees lining the roads, a close-up view of the redwood forest ecosystem, and a grove or trailhead every hundred yards or so. The turn off is at the **Big Tree Wayside,** where you can walk up to the 304-foot-high **Big Tree.** It's life was almost cut short by a homesteader who wanted to cut it down to use the stump as a dance floor. Follow the short, five-minute loop trail near the Big Tree to see the other giants in the area.

Gold Bluffs Beach

Gold Bluffs Beach (Davison Rd., three miles north of Orick off U.S. 101) is truly wild. Lonely waves pound the shore, a spikey graph of Sitka spruce top the nearby bluffs, and herds of Roosevelt elk frequently roam the wide salt-and-pepper colored sands. Prospectors found gold flakes here in 1850, giving the beach its name. But, unsurprisingly, the region was too remote and rugged to maintain a lucrative mining operation. You can access Gold Bluffs Beach by taking Davison Road. No trailers are allowed on Davison Road.

Hiking

Perhaps the single most famous hiking trail along the redwood coast is **Fern Canyon** (Davison Rd., Prairie Creek Redwoods State Park), near Gold Bluffs Beach. This hike runs through a narrow canyon carved by Home Creek. Five-fingered ferns, sword ferns, and delicate lady ferns cascade down the steep canyon walls. Droplets from seeping water sources keep the plants alive. The unusual setting was used as a dramatic backdrop in the films *Return of the Jedi* and *Jurassic Park 2*.

To get to the trailhead, take U.S. 101 three miles north of the town of Orick and then, at the Prairie Creek visitors center, turn west onto Davison Road (no trailers allowed) and travel two more miles. This rough dirt road takes you through the campground and ends at the trailhead 1.5 miles later.

A short one-mile loop trail climbs out of the canyon, surrounded by the park's trees, their limbs sleeved in green mosses. You can extend this hike into a longer (6.5 miles, moderate) loop by starting at the same place; when the trail intersects with James Irvine Trail, bear right and follow that spur. Bear right again onto **Clintonia Trail** and walk through a redwood grove to Miners Ridge Trail. Bear right onto Miners Ridge, an old logging road, and follow it down to the ocean. Walk 1.5 miles along Gold Bluffs Beach to complete the loop.

Miners Ridge and **James Irvine Loop** (12 miles, moderate) covers some of the same ground but starts from the visitors center instead of the Fern Canyon trailhead, avoiding the rough dirt terrain of Davison Road. Start out on **James Irvine Trail** and bear right when you can, following the trail all the way until it joins Fern Canyon Trail. Turn left when you get to the coast and walk along Gold Bluffs Beach for 1.5 miles. Then make a left onto the Clintonia Trail and head back toward the visitors center.

If you're starting at the visitors center but don't want to do the entire 12-mile loop, you can cut this hike roughly in half. When you get to the Clintonia Trail on your way out to the coast, make a left instead of continuing on the James Irvine Trail. This will take you over to Miners Ridge, where you make another left to loop back to the starting point, for a total of about six miles. This is a pleasant hike with plenty of great trees; the drawback is that you don't get to see Fern Canyon.

If you're hiking the **California Coastal Trail** (www.californiacoastaltrail.info), you can do a leg here at Prairie Creek. The Coastal Trail runs along the northern coast of this park. Another way to get to the campground is via the **Ossagon Creek Trail** (north end of Newton B. Drury Dr., 2 miles round-trip, moderate). It's not long, but the steep grade makes it a tough haul in spots, and the stunning trees along the way make it worth the effort.

Camping

The **Elk Prairie Campground** (127011 Newton B. Drury Dr., Orick, campground 707/488-2171, reservations 800/444-7275, www.

reserveamerica.com, vehicles $35, hikers and cyclists $5) has 75 sites for tents or RVs and a full range of comfortable camping amenities. You can get a shower and purchase wood for your fire ring. Several campsites are wheelchair-accessible, so be sure to ask for one if you need it when you reserve your site. A big campfire area is north of the campground, an easy walk for campers interested in the evening programs put on by rangers and volunteers.

For a sand camping experience, head out to **Gold Bluffs Beach Campground** (Davison Rd., 3 miles north of Orick, www.nps.gov/redw, no reservations, $35/regular sites, $20/environmental sites). There are 26 sites for tents or RVs and 3 environmental sites. Amenities include flush toilets, water, solar showers, and wide ocean views. The surf can be quite dangerous here, so be extremely careful if you go in the water.

Backcountry camping is allowed in Prairie Creek, but only in two designated camping areas, Ossagon Creek and Miners Ridge (3 sites each, $5). Permits are available at the campground kiosk or the Prairie Creek visitors center (Newton B. Drury Dr., 707/488-2171, usually daily 9am-5pm).

Getting There
Prairie Creek Redwoods is located 50 miles north of Eureka and 25 miles south of Crescent City on U.S. 101. Newton B. Drury Drive traverses the park and can be accessed from U.S. 101 north or south.

DEL NORTE COAST REDWOODS STATE PARK
South of Crescent City, **Del Norte Coast Redwoods State Park** (Mill Creek Campground Rd., off U.S. 101, 707/465-7335, www.parks.ca.gov, $8) encompasses a variety of ecosystems, including eight miles of wild coastline, second-growth redwood forest, and virgin old-growth forests. One of the largest in this system of parks, Del Norte is a great place to get lost in the backcountry with just your knapsack and your fishing rod, exploring the meandering branches of Mill Creek.

Hiking
Guided tours, nature trails, and wheelchair-accessible trails and campgrounds are all available at Del Norte. You'll want to dress in layers to hike as it can get down into the 40s even in summer. There are several rewarding yet gentle and short excursions that start and end in the Mill Creek Campground.

The **Trestle Loop Trail** (1 mile, easy) begins across from the campfire center in the campground. Notice the trestles and other artifacts along the way; the loop follows the route of a defunct railroad from the logging era. It's okay to eat the berries along this path; just keep in mind that bears and other animals like them as much as you do, so the more abundant the food, the more likely you'll have company. If you want more after this brief walk, take the nearby **Nature Loop Trail** (1 mile, easy), which begins near the campground entrance gate. This trail features interpretive signage to help you learn about the varieties of impressive trees you'll be passing.

These coastal parks are a cherished destination for serious hikers as well as sightseers, so it is possible to get a great workout along with the scenery. The northern section of the great **California Coastal Trail** (CCT, www.californiacoastaltrail.info) runs right through Del Norte Coast Redwoods State Park. The trail has been under development since 1972 and is ultimately envisioned as a 1,200-mile pathway along beaches and forests all the way from the Oregon border to the Mexican border. Not all of it will be completed for some time to come, but the parts available for use in Del Norte offer a great illustration of what the project is meant to be. The Coastal Trail is reasonably well marked; look for signs with the CCT logo.

The "last chance" section of the California Coastal Trail (Enderts Beach-Damnation Creek, 14 miles, strenuous) makes a challenging day hike. To reach the trailhead, turn west from U.S. 101 onto Enderts Beach Road in Del Norte, three miles south of Crescent City. Drive 2.3 miles to the end of the road, where the trail begins.

The trail follows the historic route of U.S.

101 south to Enderts Beach. You'll walk through fields of wildflowers and groves of trees twisted by the wind and saltwater. Eventually, the trail climbs about 900 feet to an overlook with a great view of Enderts Beach. At just over two miles, the trail enters Del Norte Coast Redwoods State Park, where it meanders through Anson Grove's redwood, fir, and Sitka spruce trees. At 4.5 miles, cross Damnation Creek on a footbridge, and at 6.1 miles, cross the Damnation Creek Trail. (For a longer hike, take the four-mile round-trip side excursion down to the beach and back.) After seven miles, a flight of steps leads up to milepost 15.6 on U.S. 101. At this point, you can turn around and return the way you came, making for a gloriously varied day hike of about 14 miles round-trip.

One alternative is to make this a point-to-point hike, either by dropping a car off at one end to get you back at the end of the day, or by having one group of hikers start at each end of the trail and exchange keys at a central meeting point.

If you've made arrangements for a lift back at the end of the day, you can continue on to the DeMartin section of the Coastal Trail. From here, descend through a lush grove of ferns and take a bridge over a tributary of Wilson Creek, enjoying views of the rocky coast far below. The wildflowers continue as you enter Redwood National Park and wander through the grasslands of DeMartin Prairie. The southern trailhead (where you pick up your vehicle if you're doing the trail one-way north-south) is at the Wilson Creek Picnic Area on the east side of U.S. 101 at the north end of DeMartin Bridge.

Camping

The **Mill Creek campground** (U.S. 101, 7 miles south of Crescent City, 800/444-7275, www.reserveamerica.com, May 1-Sept. 7, vehicles $35, hikers and cyclists $5) is in an attractive setting along Mill Creek. There are 145 sites for RVs and tents, and facilities include restrooms and fire pits. Feel free to bring your camper to the Mill Creek campground; it has spots for RVs and a dump station on-site. Call

in advance to reserve a spot and to be sure that your camper does not exceed the park's length limit. There are no designated backcountry campsites in Del Norte, and backcountry camping is not allowed.

Information and Services

Del Norte State Park has no visitors center, but you can get information from the **Crescent City Information Center** (1111 2nd St., Crescent City, 707/465-7335, spring-fall daily 9am-5pm, winter daily 9am-4pm). Minimal restroom facilities are available at the Del Norte campgrounds, and the park has an RV dump station but no RV hookups.

Getting There

Del Norte Coast Redwoods is located seven miles south of Crescent City on U.S. 101. The park entrance is on Hamilton Road, east of U.S. 101.

JEDEDIAH SMITH REDWOODS STATE PARK

The best redwood grove in the old growth of **Jedediah Smith Redwoods State Park** (U.S. 199, 9 miles east of Crescent City, 707/465-7335, www.parks.ca.gov, $8 per vehicle) is the **Stout Memorial Grove.** This bunch of coastal redwood trees is, as advertised, stout—although the grove was named for a person, not for the size of the trees. These old giants make humans feel small as they wander in the grove. These are some of the biggest and oldest trees on the North Coast and were somehow spared the loggers' saws. Another great thing about this grove is the lack of visitors, since its far-north latitude makes it harder to reach than some of the other big redwood groves in California.

Visitors Centers

There are two visitors centers in Jedediah Smith, about five minutes apart. Both offer similar information and include materials about all of the nearby parks. One is the **Jedediah Smith Visitors Center** (U.S. 101, Hiouchi, 707/458-3496, summer daily

SAVE THE REDWOODS

The stereotype of a tree-hugging conservationist usually brings to mind dirty, long-haired college students living on tarp-covered platforms and tying themselves to trees. Many visitors (and heck, residents) of California might imagine that it was a bunch of dreadlocked hippies and starving artists that saved the huge swaths of redwoods lining the North Coast region.

Nothing could be further from the truth. The California redwoods were saved by some very rich people.

Powerful rich white men poured their power, political connections, and, in some cases, millions of their own dollars into a group called the **Save the Redwoods League** (www.savetheredwoods.org). The three founders were a U.C. professor named John Merriam and fellow conservationists Madison Grant and Henry F. Osborn. After surveying the destruction of the forests surrounding brand-new U.S. 101 in 1917, the three men decided that something had to be done. And thus the League was born.

For over 90 years, the Save the Redwoods League has aggressively pursued the conservation of redwood forests in California. Using high-level political connections, the League successfully lobbied the U.S. government to create Redwood National Park and to expand the territory protected by Sequoia National Park. The league is also a major player at the state level, creating and expanding state parks all over the landscape.

So how did they get hold of all those groves? They bought them. Large donations plus the resources of League members have given the League the ability to buy thousands of acres of redwood forest, then donate them to various parks. They're still doing it to this very day, and in the 21st century the League has made several major purchases to expand Sequoia National Park, Redwood National Park, and several state parks.

Got some spare change in your ashtray? You can donate to Save the Redwoods and help the group preserve and expand California's fabulous redwoods. Donate your life savings, and they might even name a grove after you! (No promises though.)

9am-5pm, mid Sept.-mid May closed) and the other is the **Hiouchi Information Center** (U.S. 199, Hiouchi, 707/458-3294, summer daily 9am-5pm, fall-spring hours vary).

Hiking

The trails running through the trees make for wonderfully cool and shady summer hiking. Many trails run along the river and the creeks, offering a variety of ecosystems and plenty of lush scenery to enjoy. Wherever you hike, stay on the established trails. Wandering into the forest, you can trample the delicate and shallow redwood root systems, unintentionally damaging the trees you're here to visit.

The **Simpson Reed Trail** (U.S. 199, 6 miles east of Crescent City, 1 mile, easy) takes you from U.S. 199 down to the banks of the Smith River.

To get a good view of the Smith River, hike the **Hiouchi Trail** (2 miles, moderate). From the Hiouchi Information Center and campgrounds on U.S. 199, cross the Summer Footbridge and then follow the river north. The Hiouchi Trail then meets the Hatton Loop Trail and leads away from the river and into the forest.

If you're looking for a longer and more aggressive trek, try the **Mill Creek Trail** (7.5 miles round-trip, difficult). A good place to start is at the Summer Footbridge. The trail then follows the creek down to the unpaved Howland Hill Road.

If it's redwoods you're looking for, take the **Boy Scout Tree Trail** (5.2 miles, moderate). To get to the trailhead, you have to drive a rugged unpaved road for a couple of miles, but there are plenty of impressive trees to enjoy. The trail is usually quiet, with few hikers, and the gargantuan forest will make you feel truly tiny. About three miles into the trail, you'll come to a fork. If you've got time, take both forks: first the left, which takes you to the small, mossy, and very green Fern Falls, and then the right, which takes you to the eponymous Boy Scout Tree, one of the impressively huge redwoods.

Boating and Swimming

You'll find two boat launches in the park: one at Society Hole and one adjacent to the Summer Footbridge, which is only open in winter. Down by the River Beach Trail, you'll find **River Beach** (immediately west of the Hiouchi Information Center), a popular spot for swimming in the river. Swimming is allowed throughout the park, but be very careful—rivers and creeks move unpredictably, and you might not notice deep holes until you're on them. Enjoy the cool water, but keep a close eye on children and other loved ones to ensure a safe time.

Fishing

With the Smith River and numerous feeder creeks running through Jed Smith, it's not surprising that fishing is one of the most popular activities. Chilly winter fishing draws a surprising number of anglers to vie for king salmon up to 30 pounds and steelhead up to 20 pounds. Seasons for both species run October-February. In the summer you can cast into the river to catch cutthroat trout.

Camping

The **Jedediah Smith Campground** (U.S. 199, Hiouchi, 800/444-7275, www.reserveamerica. com, vehicles $35, hike-in or cycle-in primitive sites $5) is beautifully situated on the banks of Smith River, with most sites near the River Beach Trail (immediately west of the Hiouchi Information Center). There are 106 RV and tent sites. Facilities include plenty of restrooms, fire pits, and coin-operated showers. Reservations are advised, especially for summer and holiday weekends. The campground is open year-round, but reservations are accepted only Memorial Day-Labor Day. Jedediah Smith has no designated backcountry campsites, and camping outside the developed campgrounds is not allowed. If you're backpacking, check at one of the visitors centers for help in finding the nearest place to camp overnight.

Getting There

Jedediah Smith Redwoods State Park (U.S. 199, 9 miles east of Crescent City, 707/458-3018, www.parks.ca.gov, $8 per vehicle) is northeast of Crescent City along the Smith River, next door to the immense Smith River National Recreation Area (U.S. 199 west of Hiouchi). You can get there by taking U.S. 199 nine miles east of Crescent City.

Crescent City

The northernmost city on the California coast perches on the bay that provides its name. Cool and windswept, Crescent City is a perfect place to put on a parka, stuff your hands deep into your pockets, and wander along a wide, beautiful beach. The small city also has a vibrant surf scene centered around South Beach, which frequently has good waves for longboarders.

Crescent City is also known for surviving tsunamis. In 1964, a tsunami caused by an Alaskan earthquake wiped out 29 city blocks and killed 11 people. It was the most severe tsunami on the U.S. West Coast in modern history. In 2011, the devastating earthquake in Japan resulted in a tsunami that laid waste to

the city's harbor. The old rusted warning sirens on the tops of the city's utility poles still work; when they sound, there's a chance of massive waves coming to shore.

Due to the depressed logging and fishing economy, Crescent City's downtown has its fair share of shuttered businesses. But if you're looking for an inexpensive hotel room to use as a base to explore the nearby redwoods or the area's impressive beaches, a night or two in Crescent City will fit the bill.

SIGHTS
Point St. George

Wild, lonely, beautiful **Point St. George** (end

of Washington Blvd.) epitomizes the glory of the North Coast of California. Walk out onto the cliffs to take in the deep blue sea, wild salt- and flower-scented air and craggy cliffs and beaches. On a clear day, you can see all the way to Oregon. Short steep trails lead across wild beach prairie land down to broad, flat, nearly deserted beaches. In spring-summer wildflowers bloom on the cliffs, and swallows nest in the cluster of buildings on the point. On rare and special clear days, you can almost make out the **St. George Reef Lighthouse** alone on its perch far out in the Pacific.

(Battery Point Lighthouse

Located on an island just north of Crescent City Harbor, the **Battery Point Lighthouse** (end of A St., 707/464-3089, daily Apr.-Sept., daily tides permitting, 10am-4pm, Oct.-Mar. Sat.-Sun. tides permitting 10am-4pm, adults $3, children 8-15 $1) is only accessible at low tide, when a rocky spit littered with tide pools emerges, serving as a walkway for visitors. The 1856 lighthouse's current keepers reside on the island in one-month shifts; they also lead tours. You'll see a Fresnel lens and a working clock that was used by Battery Point's first lighthouse keeper. After viewing the two resi- dential floors of the building, the docent leads any adventurous visitors up a metal ladder through a small hole into the lantern room, where you'll be able to feel the heat of the still working light just feet away. On a clear day, you'll also be able to see the pencil-like outline of the St. George Reef Lighthouse in the distance. St. George is situated on a small, wave-washed rock seven miles from shore, and its dangerous location resulted in the deaths of four keepers who worked there.

Ocean World

Are the kids bored with all the gorgeous scen- ery? A great family respite is **Ocean World** (304 U.S. 101 S., 707/464-4900, www.ocean- worldonline.com, summer daily 9am-9pm, winter daily 10am-6pm, adults $10, children $6). Tours of the small sea park depart about every 15 minutes and last about 40 minutes.

Featured attractions are the shark petting tank, the 500,000-gallon aquarium, and the sea lion show. After the tour, take a stroll through the immense souvenir shop, which sells gifts of all sizes, shapes, and descriptions, many with nau- tical themes.

Del Norte County Historical Society Museum

The **Del Norte County Historical Society Museum** (577 H St., 707/464-3922, www. delnortehistory.org, Apr.-Sept. Mon.-Sat. 10am-4pm, Oct.-Mar. by appointment, free) provides an educational respite from the chilly sea breezes. The Historical Society maintains this small museum that features the local his- tory of both the Native Americans who were once the only inhabitants of Del Norte County and the encroaching white settlers. Featured ex- hibits include the wreck of the *Brother Jonathan* at Point St. George, the story of the 1964 tsu- nami, and artifacts of the local Yurok and Tolowa people.

ENTERTAINMENT AND EVENTS

If you're looking for varied and rocking nightlife, Crescent City is not your town, but a few options exist for insomniacs. Most of the action after 9pm is at **Elk Valley Casino** (2500 Howland Hill Rd., 707/464-1020 or 888/574-2744, www.elkvalleycasino.com, daily 24 hours) at the eastern edge of town. Elk Valley is a bit more upscale than other local Native American casinos, with genuine aluminum-siding walls, poker and blackjack tables, a VIP card room, and a small non- smoking slots area. The on-site restaurant is the **Full House Bar & Grill** (Sun.-Thurs. 7am-10pm, Fri.-Sat. 7am-11pm, $7-29); a late-night food menu (daily 7am-2am) is available from the bar.

The **Tsunami Lanes Bowling Center** (760 L St., 707/464-4323, www.tsunamilanes.com, Mon.-Fri. noon-10pm, Sat. noon-midnight, adults $3 per game, seniors and children $2) is a straight-up bowling alley, serving beer and greasy fries to all comers late into the evening.

Crescent City's Battery Point Lighthouse

Theater

The **Del Norte Association for Cultural Awareness** (Crescent Elk Auditorium, 994 G St., 707/464-1336, www.dnaca.net) hosts several live musical acts and other performances each year and provides a community arts calendar. Check this year's schedule for upcoming shows.

Cinema

If all else fails, you can take in a first-run movie at the **Crescent City Cinemas** (375 M St., 707/570-8438, www.catheatres.com). Or even better, take in a movie in an old-fashioned drive-through theater at **Red's Crescent Drive-In Theatre** (four miles north of Crescent City on Elk Valley Crossroads, 707/464-1813, $12/vehicle).

Events

For almost 50 years, the Yurok people have held a festival to honor a creature most precious to them: the mighty salmon. The **Klamath Salmon Festival** (www.yuroktribe.org) takes place in August each year and includes a parade, live music, games, and, of course, salmon dinners served all day.

Each August since the early 1980s, the **Crescent City Triathlon** (707/465-3995, www.crescentcitytriathlon.com, adults $30-50, children $20-25) has challenged participants of all ages. This triathlon is a 5K run, a 500-yard swim, and a 12-mile bike ride (c'mon—you can do that). There's also a duathlon, which involves a run, a bike ride, and then another run; and there's a triathlon for kids that varies in intensity by age group, making it possible for anyone ages 5-12 to join the fun.

SPORTS AND RECREATION

Beaches

The sands of Crescent City are a beachcomber's paradise. Wide, flat, sandy expanses invite strolling, running, and just sitting to contemplate the broad crashing Pacific. **South Beach** (Hwy. 1 between Anchor Way and Sand Mine Rd.), as advertised, is located at the south end of town. Long, wide, and flat, it's perfect for a romantic stroll, as long as you're bundled up. The adventurous and chill-resistant can try surfing and boogie boarding. Farther south, **Crescent Beach** (Enderts Rd.) is two miles south of town. It's a wide, sandy beach. Down a half-mile dirt trail, **Enderts Beach** (Enderts Rd.) is a superb beach nestled along the coast south of Crescent City. This pocket beach has a creek flowing into the ocean and an onshore rock arch.

It might look tempting on rare sunny days, but swimming from the beaches of Crescent City is not for the faint of heart. The water is icy cold, the shores are rocky, and as elsewhere in Northern California, undertow and rip currents can be dangerous. No lifeguards patrol these beaches, so you are on your own.

Bird-Watching

Birders flock to Crescent City because the diverse climates and habitats nourish a huge variety of avian residents. The parks and preserves have become destinations for enthusiasts looking for "lifers" hard to find anyplace else. Right in town, check out **Battery Point Lighthouse Park** and **Point St. George.** For a rare view of an Aleutian goose or a peregrine falcon, journey to **Tolowa Dunes State Park** (1375 Elk Valley Rd., 707/465-2145, www.parks.ca.gov, daily sunrise-sunset, free), specifically the shores of Lake Earl and Kellog Beach. South of town, **Enderts Beach** is home to another large bird habitat.

Fishing and Whale-Watching

Anglers on the North Coast can choose between excellent deep-sea fishing and exciting river trips. The Pacific yields ling cod, snapper, and salmon, while the rivers are famous for chinook (king) salmon, steelhead, and cutthroat trout. Mammal-loving travelers can choose whale-watching over fishing. The *Tally Ho II* (1685 Del Mar Rd., at the harbor, 707/464-1236) is available for a variety of deep-sea fishing trips (May-Oct., half-day trip $100 pp), whale-watching (Feb.-Mar., 3-hour trip $50), or a combination of the two.

© STUART THORNTON

Enderts Beach

River fishers have a wealth of guides to choose from. **Ken Cunningham Guide Service** (50 Hunter Creek, Klamath, 707/391-7144, www.salmonslayer.net, $200-250) will take you on a full-day fishing trip; the price includes bait, tackle, and the boat. **North Coast Fishing Adventures** (1657 Childrens Ave., McKinleyville, 707/498-4087 or 707/839-8127, www.norcalriverfishing.com, $200 pp, minimum $400 per day) covers the Klamath and Smith Rivers as well as smaller waterways.

Hiking

The redwood forests that nearly meet the wide sandy beaches make the Crescent City area a fabulous place to hike. The hikes at **Point St. George** aren't strenuous and provide stunning views of the coastline and surrounding landscape. **Tolowa Dunes State Park** (1375 Elk Valley Rd., 707/465-2145, www.parks.ca.gov, daily sunrise-sunset, free), north of Point St. George, offers miles of trails winding through forests, across beaches, and meandering along the shores of Lake Earl.

Horseback Riding

The rugged land surrounding Crescent City looks even prettier from the back of a horse. Casual riders enjoy a guided riding adventure through redwoods or along the ocean with **Crescent Trail Rides** (2002 Moorehead Rd., 707/951-5407, www.crescenttrailrides.com, 1.5 hours $60, 4 hours $160). Under the same management, **Fort Dick Stable** (2002 Moorehead Rd., 707/951-5407, www.fortdickstable.com) offers boarding and riding lessons.

A great place to ride is **Tolowa Dunes State Park** (1375 Elk Valley Rd., 707/465-2145, www.parks.ca.gov, daily sunrise-sunset, free), which maintains 20 miles of trails accessible to horses. Serious equestrians with their own mounts can ride in to a campsite with corrals at the north end of the park off Lower Lake Road.

Surfing

While Crescent City is a long way from the legendary Southern California surf scene, the northernmost coastal city in California has a collection of surf breaks. Pioneering big wave surfer Greg Noll even lives in Crescent City. Just south of the harbor you'll find the most popular break in town, **South Beach** (Hwy. 1 between Anchor Way and Sand Mine Rd.), with peeling waves perfect for longboarders and beginners. It was once home to the Annual Noll Longboard Classic. North of town, **Point St. George** (end of Washington Blvd.) has a reef and point break that comes alive during winter. Run over to **South Beach Outfitters** (128 Anchor Way, 707/464-2963 or 877/330-7873, http://southbeachoutfitters.com, summer daily 10am-5pm, winter Wed.-Sun. 10am-5pm, board rental $25, wetsuit rental $10) to rent a board and wetsuit.

ACCOMMODATIONS

Lodgings in Crescent City are affordable even during the midsummer high season and can be surprisingly comfortable.

The aptly named **Curly Redwood Lodge** (701 U.S. 101 S., 707/464-2137, www.curlyredwoodlodge.com, $70-95) is constructed of a single rare curly redwood tree. You'll get to see the lovely color and grain of the tree in your large, simply decorated guest room. A 1950s feel pervades this friendly unpretentious motel even though it offers free Wi-Fi and is upgrading to flat screen TVs in every room. Right on U.S. 101, you can walk to South Beach or the Crescent City Harbor.

Few frills decorate the family-owned **Pacific Inn** (220 M. St., 707/464-9553 or 800/977-9553, $52-73), but the guest rooms are clean, inexpensive, and comfortable. Its central downtown location makes for easy access to restaurants, museums, and points of interest.

The **Lighthouse Inn** (681 U.S. 101 S., 707/464-3993 or 877/464-3993, www.lighthouse101.com, $89-145) has an elegant but whimsical lobby filled with dolphins and dollhouses to welcome guests, and the enthusiastic staff can help with restaurant recommendations and sights. Stylish appointments and bold colors grace each guest room. Corner suites with oversize whirlpool tubs make a perfect romantic retreat for couples at a reasonable nightly rate, while standard double rooms are downright cheap, given their comfort.

The **Anchor Beach Inn** (880 U.S. 101 S., 800/837-4116, www.anchorbeachinn.com, $59-118), at the south end of town, offers great access to South Beach, the harbor, and several good seafood restaurants. The ocean views overlook a wide swath of asphalt RV park, but the guest rooms have attractive decor and are clean and well maintained; continental breakfast and Internet access are included.

The best lodging location in town may be the **◖ Cottage by the Sea** (205 S. A St., 707/951-1448 or 877/642-2254, www.vrbo.com, $135). Downtown and right on the coast, both the honeymoon cottage and the house overlook the Battery Point Lighthouse. At this nontraditional B&B, the owner cooks breakfast on request. Special rates are available for stays of at least three days.

FOOD

Not surprisingly, seafood is standard fare in Crescent City, but family restaurants and one or two ethnic eateries add some appealing variety.

American

Enjoy an impressive variety of fresh and healthy food at **The Good Harvest Cafe** (575 U.S. 101 S., 707/465-6028, Mon.-Sat. 7:30am-9pm, Sun. 8am-8pm, $10-35). It serves the best breakfast in town, with vegetarian options like tofu rancheros and veggie frittata. Steak and lobster dinner is at the high end of the dinner menu, which also includes burgers, pasta, vegetarian entrées, and big salads. Kitschy Native American decorations abound inside and out.

Fishermans Restaurant (700 U.S. 101 S., 707/465-3474, daily 6am-9pm, $11-26) is a casual place to grab a bite. You can walk in wearing jeans and sandy sneakers. The diverse dinner menu includes fresh local seafood offerings. Breakfasts feature biscuits and gravy, pancakes, and thick juicy bacon, all delicious—and big enough—to sustain you through a long day of hauling nets.

Coffee Shops and Markets

The **Java Hut** (437 U.S. 101 N., 707/465-4439, daily 5am-10pm, $5) is a drive-through and walk-up coffee stand that serves a wide array of coffee drinks. Beware of long lines of locals during the morning hours.

The small, family-owned, award-winning **Rumiano Cheese Co.** (511 9th St., 707/465-1535 or 866/328-2433, www.rumianocheese.com, June-Dec. Mon.-Fri. 9am-5pm, Sat. 9am-3pm, Jan.-May Mon.-Fri. 9am-5pm) has been part of Crescent City since 1921. Come to the tasting room for the cheese and stay for, well, more cheese. The dry jack cheese is a particular favorite, though lots of varieties are available.

Like many California towns, Crescent City runs a **farmers market** (Del Norte County Fairgrounds, 451 U.S. 101 N., 707/460-3537, June-Oct. Sat. 9am-1pm). While the harvest season is more restricted here than points south, veggie lovers can still choose from an array of fresh local produce all summer long.

Seafood

Northwood's Restaurant (675 U.S. 101 S., 707/465-5656, daily 6am-9pm, $8-20) prides itself on serving the freshest fish available, and in Crescent City that can mean the fillet you're eating for dinner was caught that very morning by a local fishing boat. The varied menu also includes imported exotic fish plus a number of land-based entrées to appeal to every palate.

For better seafood still at a reasonable price, the best bet is **The Chart Room** (130 Anchor Way, 707/464-5993, www.chartroomcrescentcity.com, summer Mon. 11am-4pm, Tues.-Sun. 6:30am-8pm, winter Thurs.-Sun. 7am-7pm, $10-23). It's very casual, the food is excellent, and it's right on the ocean, so you can watch sea lions cavort on the pier while you eat. If anyone in your party is not a seafood lover, the lasagna is excellent.

Thai

A Thai restaurant in Crescent City? Believe it. The **Thai House** (105 N. St., 707/464-2427, Sun.-Thurs. 11am-9pm, Fri.-Sat. 11am-10pm,

$10-15) does passable Thai food including curries and pad Thai.

INFORMATION AND SERVICES

The **Crescent City and Del Norte County Chamber of Commerce Visitors Center** (1001 Front St., 707/464-3174 or 800/343-8300, www.exploredelnorte.com, Mon.-Fri. 10am-4pm) is a good place to visit when you arrive. You'll find knowledgeable staffers who can advise you on "secret" local sights as well as the bigger attractions advertised in the myriad brochures lining the walls.

Also in town is the **Crescent City Information Center** (1111 2nd St., 707/465-7335, spring-fall daily 9am-5pm, winter daily 9am-4pm) run by Redwood National and State Parks. This friendly place has maps, souvenirs, and rangers who can chat about hiking, camping, and exploring the parks.

The Daily Triplicate (707/464-2141, www.triplicate.com), the local newspaper of Crescent City, is published Tuesday, Thursday, and Saturday. You can pick up a Del Norte County Map and a copy of *101 Things to Do in Del Norte/Southern Oregon* (www.101things.com) at the visitors center and many local businesses.

GETTING THERE AND AROUND

The main routes in and out of town are U.S. 101 and U.S. 199. Both are well maintained but are twisty in spots, so take care, especially at night. From San Francisco, the drive to Crescent City is about 350 miles (6.5 hours). It is 85 miles (under two hours) from Eureka north to Crescent City on U.S. 101. Traffic isn't a big issue in Crescent City, and parking is free and easy to find throughout town.

Jack McNamara Field (CEC, 5 miles northwest of town, 707/464-7288, www.fly-cec.com) is also called Del Norte County Airport and is the only airport in Crescent City. United Express has daily nonstop flights to San Francisco and Sacramento.

Redwood Coast Transit (RCT, 707/464-6400, www.redwoodcoasttransit.org, adults $0.75, senior and disabled $0.50, punch passes $10) handles bus travel in and around Crescent City. Make sure to have exact change handy. Four in-town routes and a coastal bus from Smith River to Arcata provide ample public-transit options for travelers without cars. Pick up a schedule at the visitors center (1001 Front St.) or local stores for current fares and times.

MOON SPOTLIGHT MENDOCINO & REDWOOD COUNTRY

Avalon Travel
a member of the Perseus Books Group
1700 Fourth Street
Berkeley, CA 94710, USA
www.moon.com

Editor: Kevin McLain
Series Manager: Kathryn Ettinger
Copy Editor: Naomi Adler Dancis
Graphics and Production Coordinator:
  Domini Dragoone
Map Editor: Albert Angulo
Cartographers: Chris Henrick, Andy Butkovic, Kaitlin
  Jaffe, and Kat Bennett
Indexer: Rachel Kuhn

ISBN-13: 978-1-61238-980-6

Text © 2014 by Stuart Thornton and Avalon Travel.
Maps © 2014 by Avalon Travel.
All rights reserved.

Front cover photo: Early morning light illuminates dramatic clouds above the Point Arena Headland and Lighthouse, © kjschoen / istockphoto.com
Title page photo: Redwood forest, © Matt Tilgham/123RF

Printed in the United States

ABOUT THE AUTHOR

© SHANE DOLBIER

Stuart Thornton

Stuart Thornton first fell in love with the California coast when he got a job at the Big Sur Ranger Station. At work, he provided visitors with all sorts of information about the region, from the best places to camp to the best places to eat. On his days off, he took his own advice and regularly sought out the best local spots for hiking, backpacking, surfing, and snorkeling.

Stuart later moved to nearby Monterey to become a staff writer for the *Monterey County Weekly*, and he now works as a freelance writer for a range of publications, from *National Geographic Education* to *Relix Magazine*.

Stuart has traveled the length and breadth of the California coastline. When not on the road searching for the next great secluded beach, uncrowded wave, or quirky coastal attraction, he lives in Marina, California.

CPSIA information can be obtained at www.ICGtesting.com
Printed in the USA
LVOW01s1520150814

399317LV00001B/1/P

9 781612 389806